Collins

KS3
Science
Year 7

Ian Honeysett, Sam Holyman and Lynn Pharaoh

How to use this book

Each Year 7 topic is presented on a two-page spread

Organise your knowledge with concise explanations and examples

Key points highlight fundamental ideas

Test your retrieval skills by trying the accompanying questions for the topic

Mixed questions further test retrieval skills after all topics have been covered

Scientific skills section provides further knowledge and explanations of scientific ideas and investigative skills

Answers are provided to all questions at the back of the book

ACKNOWLEDGEMENTS

The authors and publisher are grateful to the copyright holders for permission to use quoted materials and images.

Every effort has been made to trace copyright holders and obtain their permission for the use of copyright material. The authors and publisher will gladly receive information enabling them to rectify any error or omission in subsequent editions. All facts are correct at time of going to press.

All images ©Shutterstock and HarperCollins*Publishers*

Published by Collins
An imprint of HarperCollins*Publishers* Limited
1 London Bridge Street
London SE1 9GF

HarperCollinsPublishers
Macken House, 39/40 Mayor Street Upper,
Dublin 1, D01 C9W8, Ireland

© HarperCollins*Publishers* Limited 2023
ISBN 9780008598679
First published 2023
10 9 8 7 6 5 4 3 2 1

All rights reserved. No part of this publication may be reproduced, stored in a retrieval system, or transmitted, in any form or by any means, electronic, mechanical, photocopying, recording or otherwise, without the prior permission of Collins.

British Library Cataloguing in Publication Data.
A CIP record of this book is available from the British Library.

Authors: Ian Honeysett, Sam Holyman and Lynn Pharaoh
Publisher: Clare Souza
Commissioning: Richard Toms
Project Management: Katie Galloway
Inside Concept Design: Ian Wrigley
Layout: Rose & Thorn Creative Services Ltd
Cover Design: Sarah Duxbury
Production: Emma Wood
Printed in India by Multivista Global Pvt. Ltd

This book is produced from independently certified FSC™ paper to ensure responsible forest management.

For more information visit:
www.harpercollins.co.uk/green

Contents

1 Biology

What are living things made of?	4
How can we see cells?	6
How are unicellular and multicellular organisms different?	8
How does reproduction happen in plants?	10
How does the human reproductive system function?	12
How do humans reproduce?	14
What is a healthy diet?	16
What is the human digestive system?	18
What is the human breathing system?	20
What is diffusion?	22
How can lifestyle affect disease?	24

2 Chemistry

How do you work safely in a laboratory?	26
How do you record experiments?	28
How can you classify a substance?	30
What is a solution?	32
How can you separate mixtures?	34
How are separation techniques used in industry?	36
What is the Periodic Table?	38
What are metals?	40
What are non-metals and metalloids?	42
What happens to mass in a chemical or physical change (1)?	44
What happens in a chemical reaction?	46
What happens in oxidation reactions?	48
What happens in a decomposition reaction?	50
What happens to mass in a chemical or physical change (2)?	52

3 Physics

What is a force?	54
What is weight?	56
How do forces interact?	58
What happens when a force is applied to elastic materials?	60
What is friction?	62
How do forces affect speed and direction?	64
What is speed?	66
What is a lever?	68
What is a moment?	70
What is a machine?	72

Mixed questions **74**

Scientific skills **78**

Answers 82

ORGANISE

1. What are living things made of?

Animal cells

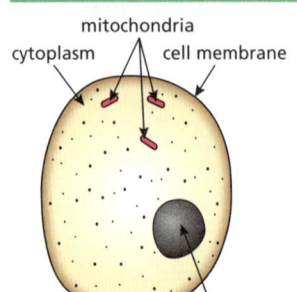

All living organisms are made of one or more units called cells. Cells have certain features in common but there are differences between plant and animal cells.

A typical animal cell has:
- a **cell membrane** that controls which substances can enter or leave the cell
- a **nucleus** that contains the genetic material (DNA) and controls the reactions occurring in the cell
- a jelly-like substance called **cytoplasm** in the rest of the cell, where many chemical reactions take place
- small structures in the cytoplasm called **mitochondria** where respiration happens.

Plant cells

Plant cells have a cell membrane, cytoplasm and mitochondria like animal cells, but also have:
- a **cell wall** outside the cell membrane which is made of cellulose and supports the cell
- structures called **chloroplasts** where photosynthesis happens (not all plant cells have chloroplasts)
- a large **vacuole** containing fluid called cell sap, which stores sugars and salts and supports the cell.

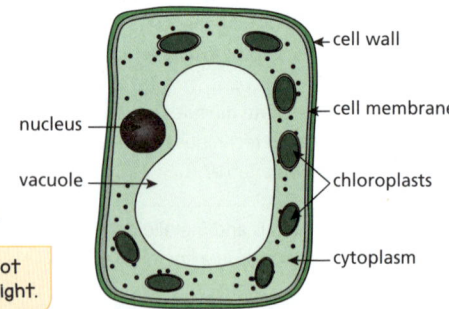

Not all plant cells have chloroplasts. Cells in the root will not have any because they do not get any sunlight.

Specialised cells

In multicellular organisms, different cells become **specialised** to do different jobs. This makes them more **efficient**. They still have the structures shown in the typical cells but have different shapes and features to allow them to do the different jobs.

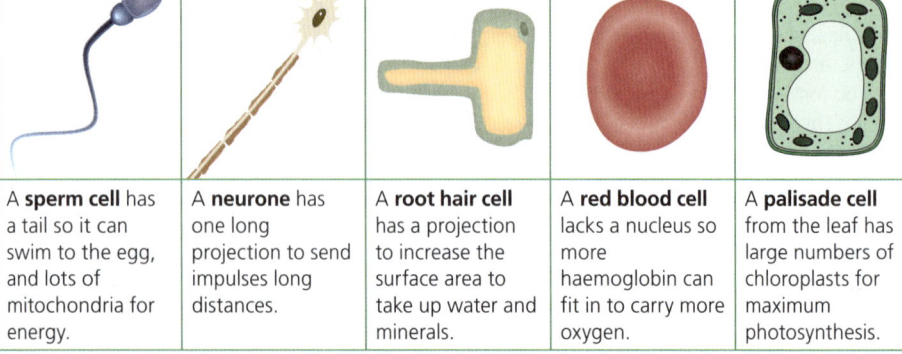

A **sperm cell** has a tail so it can swim to the egg, and lots of mitochondria for energy.	A **neurone** has one long projection to send impulses long distances.	A **root hair cell** has a projection to increase the surface area to take up water and minerals.	A **red blood cell** lacks a nucleus so more haemoglobin can fit in to carry more oxygen.	A **palisade cell** from the leaf has large numbers of chloroplasts for maximum photosynthesis.

RETRIEVE

What are living things made of?

Animal cells

1 Look at the diagram of a typical animal cell. Give the letter that labels each of these parts of the cell.

a) Cytoplasm

b) Cell membrane

c) The part of the cell that contains DNA

d) The part of the cell that controls what enters and leaves

2 What is the function of mitochondria in a cell?

....

....

Plant cells

3 What are plant cell walls made of?

....

4 What is the function of plant cell walls?

....

5 Name **two** structures found in **all** plant cells but not in animal cells.

....

6 Plant root hair cells do not have chloroplasts. Why is this?

....

....

Specialised cells

7 Different cells have different features so they are adapted for different functions.
Explain why each of these cells has these features.

a) A sperm cell has a tail.

....

....

b) A root hair cell has a projection sticking out on one side.

....

....

8 Explain why it is an advantage for multicellular organisms to have specialised cells.

....

....

Biology   5

ORGANISE

How can we see cells?

Using a microscope

Most cells are too small to see without a microscope. The main parts of the microscope are:
- two lenses that magnify the object: the **eyepiece lens** and the **objective lens**
- a **stage** with clips to hold the microscope slide
- two **focus knobs** which are used to focus the image
- a **mirror** (or light bulb) which is used to shine light through the specimen.

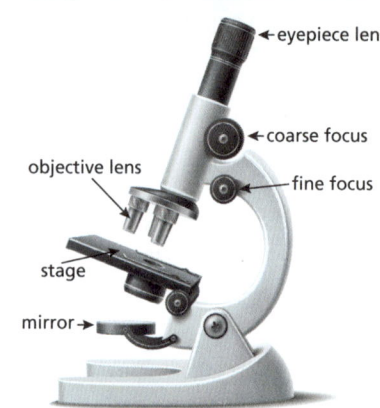

> Many biological specimens are fairly transparent, so coloured stains are used to make structures show up.

Before looking at the specimen using a microscope, the specimen needs to be prepared:

thin section of the specimen is placed onto a microscope slide

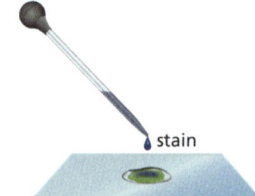

a few drops of stain are added to make structures in the specimen easier to see

a cover slip is lowered on to the specimen

Drawing and measuring cells

When making biological drawings from a microscope image there are certain rules to obey:
- make clear lines without sketching
- do not shade
- use a ruler for label lines.

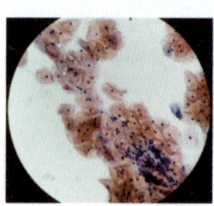

microscope image of cheek cells

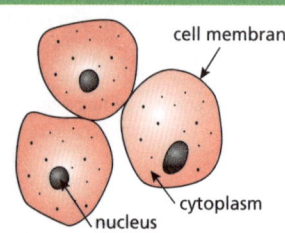

biological drawing of cheek cells

As cells are so small, they are not usually measured in centimetres or even millimetres but in **micrometres**. There are 1000 micrometres in a millimetre.

To work out the magnification of a drawing, this formula is used:

$$\text{magnification} = \frac{\text{size of the object in the drawing}}{\text{size of the object in real life}}$$

> When calculating the magnification, make sure you are using the same units for the size of the drawing and the size in real life.

RETRIEVE

1) How can we see cells?

Using a microscope

1 Why do we need to use a microscope to study cells?

....

2 Look at the diagram of the microscope.

Write down the letters that label each of these parts.

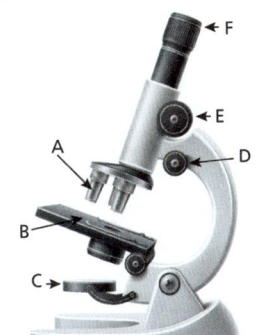

a) Objective lens ☐

b) Eyepiece lens ☐

c) The part where the microscope slide is placed ☐

d) The part that shines light through the specimen ☐

3 What is the name of each of these items used to prepare a specimen to be seen with a microscope?

a) A rectangular piece of glass that the specimen is placed on ....

b) A coloured liquid dropped onto the specimen ....

c) A thin square of glass placed on top of the specimen ....

Drawing and measuring cells

4 Look at the drawing of a cell made by a student.

Write down **two** drawing mistakes made by the student.

....

....

5 The drawing of the cell is 40 millimetres wide.

How wide is the drawing of the cell in **micrometres**?

....

6 The cell is 40 micrometres wide in real life.

Calculate the magnification of the drawing of the cell.

....

Biology 7

 # How are unicellular and multicellular organisms different?

Unicellular organisms

Unicellular organisms are made up of one single cell. All the living processes must be done by this single cell.

Bacteria are the simplest unicellular organisms. Bacteria:
- do not have a nucleus (the DNA is in the cytoplasm)
- do not have mitochondria
- have a cell membrane surrounded by a cell wall
- are much smaller than other cells.

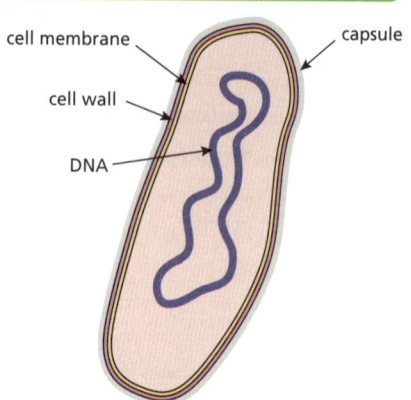

> Bacteria feed in different ways. Some make their own food, some feed on dead material and some feed on living organisms, causing disease.

Other types of unicellular organism are larger than bacteria and have a more complicated structure. Some feed more like plants, others like animals and some are like fungi.

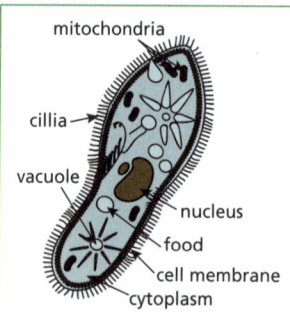	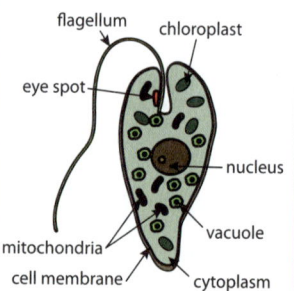	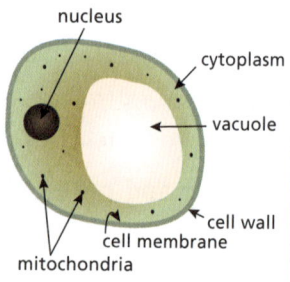
Paramecium eats small algae and moves around by beating small hairs called cilia.	**Euglena** has chloroplasts and so makes its own food like plants.	**Yeast** feeds on dead fruit and has a cell wall like fungi.

Organisation in multicellular organisms

In multicellular organisms, there are different levels of organisation:
- there are **cells** that can be specialised for different functions
- similar cells that do similar jobs are gathered into **tissues**
- different tissues are gathered to form **organs** to do a particular job
- groups of organs often work together in **systems**.

> Remember that bone and nerve are tissues, but a bone and a nerve are organs.

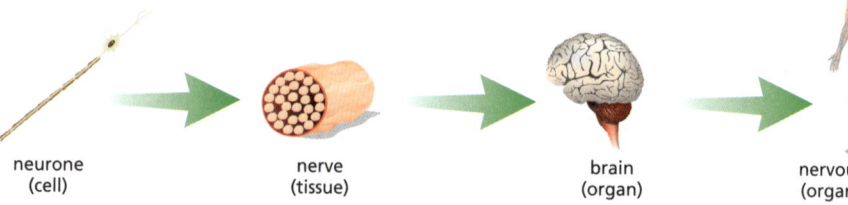

neurone (cell) → nerve (tissue) → brain (organ) → nervous system (organ system)

RETRIEVE 1: How are unicellular and multicellular organisms different?

Unicellular organisms

1 Write down **two** organelles found in other unicellular organisms but not in bacteria.

....

....

2 Where in bacteria is DNA found?

....

3 For each description, give the name of a unicellular organism.

Choose your answers from this list.

bacteria	Euglena	Paramecium	yeast

a) An organism that is covered in small hairs called cilia ....

b) An organism that has a nucleus and feeds on dead fruit ....

c) An organism that has chloroplasts ....

d) An organism that does not have a nucleus ....

4 Which of the organisms in the list in Question 3 have mitochondria?

....

Organisation in multicellular organisms

5 Write down these levels of organisation in order, starting from the simplest to the most complicated.

systems	cells	organs	tissues

....

6 Write down the level of organisation for each one of these structures.

Choose the levels from the list in Question 5.

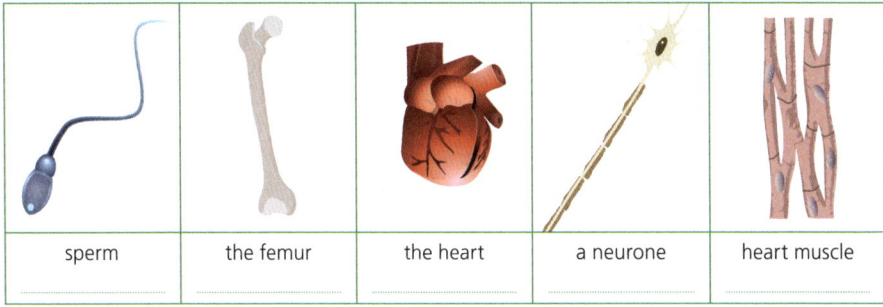

sperm	the femur	the heart	a neurone	heart muscle

Biology 9

ORGANISE

1 How does reproduction happen in plants?

Parts of a flower

Flowers are the parts of a plant that are involved in sexual reproduction. Most flowers have both male and female parts:
- the male parts are **stamens** and produce **pollen**, which contains the male sex cells
- the pollen is made in the swelling called the **anther**
- the female part of the flower is the **carpel**
- the female sex cells are made in the **ovules**, which are in the **ovaries**.

> The structures of different flowers vary quite a lot, for example, some flowers have one ovule in the ovary while others have many.

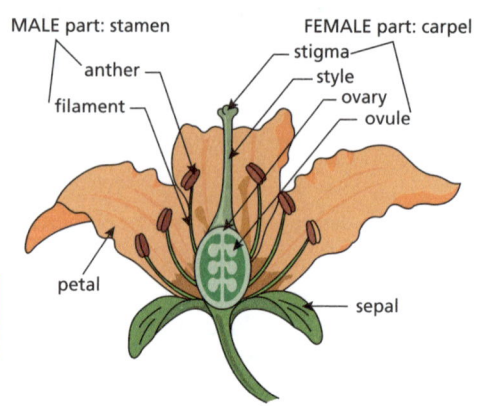

Methods of pollination

Pollination is the transfer of pollen from the anther to the stigma. The pollen can be transferred in different ways but the most common ways are by insects or by wind. Flowers are adapted for insect or wind pollination.

Insect-pollinated flowers	Wind-pollinated flowers
• Have bright coloured petals to attract insects. • Make nectar or scent to attract insects. • Anthers and stigmas are inside the flower. • Make small amounts of sticky pollen.	• Petals are usually green. • No nectar or scent. • Anthers and stigmas hang outside the flower. • Make large amounts of light pollen.

After a flower is pollinated, the pollen grain grows a tube down to the ovule.

The male gamete then passes down the tube and fertilises the female gamete.

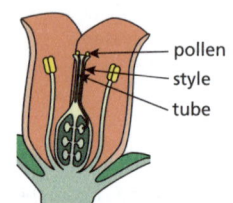

> After fertilisation, the ovule develops into a **seed** and the ovary becomes a **fruit**.

Seed dispersal

Once the seeds are ripe, they need to be released so they can grow into a new plant. It is better if they can be spread away from the parent plant. This is called **seed dispersal**. It stops the new plants competing with each other and with the parent plant.

Seeds can be dispersed in different ways:

 some seeds or fruits have hooks to cling to animals

 some plants eject the seeds themselves

 some seeds or fruits are carried by the wind

 some fruits or seeds are eaten by animals and the seeds pass out in the faeces

RETRIEVE

1) How does reproduction happen in plants?

Parts of a flower

1 Write down the name for the part of a flower that fits each description.

a) The male part of the flower ....

b) The female part of the flower ....

c) The swelling of the male part that makes pollen ....

d) The part that contains the female gamete ....

2 What do pollen grains contain?

Methods of pollination

3 What is pollination?

4 Explain why insect-pollinated flowers have bright petals.

5 Write down **one other** adaptation of insect-pollinated flowers.

6 Explain why wind-pollinated flowers make large amounts of light-weight pollen.

7 Write down **one other** adaptation of wind-pollinated flowers.

Seed dispersal

8 Fill in the blanks to complete these sentences.

After a flower is pollinated, the pollen grain grows a .... down to the ....
This allows fertilisation to happen.

After fertilisation, the ovule becomes a .... and the .... becomes a fruit.

9 Why is it important for plants to disperse their seeds?

10 A dandelion seed is attached to a very light ring of hairs.
Explain how dandelion seeds are dispersed.

Biology 11

ORGANISE 1: How does the human reproductive system function?

Female reproductive system

The female reproductive system makes female sex cells (eggs) and contains the growing foetus until it is born.
Different parts of the system have different functions:
- the **ovaries** are where the eggs are made
- the eggs are released into the **oviducts** and it is here that they may be fertilised
- the fertilised egg passes down the oviduct to the **uterus** where it will burrow into the lining to grow into a baby
- at birth, the uterus contracts and pushes the baby through a ring of muscle called the **cervix**
- the baby then passes to the outside through a muscular tube called the **vagina**.

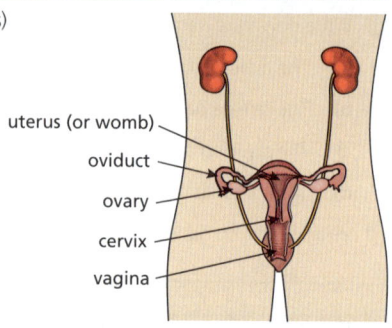

uterus (or womb)
oviduct
ovary
cervix
vagina

Male reproductive system

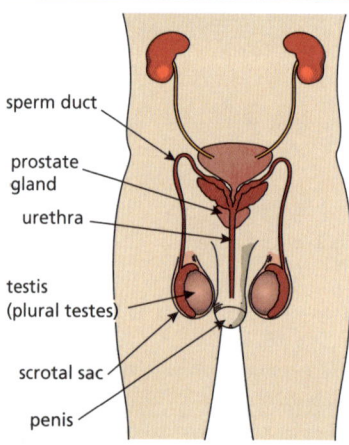

sperm duct
prostate gland
urethra
testis (plural testes)
scrotal sac
penis

The male reproductive system produces millions of male sex cells (sperm). It then delivers them into the female so that one can fertilise the egg:
- the **testes** are where the sperm are made
- the testes are in the **scrotal sac** to protect them and keep them slightly below body temperature
- the sperm move along the **sperm duct** by muscular contractions
- liquid is added to the sperm by the **prostate gland**
- the sperm then pass along the **urethra**
- they then exit the **penis** into the female's vagina during sexual intercourse.

> Be careful of the spelling of the urethra. The word is similar to ureter, which is a tube that brings urine to the bladder.

Changes at puberty

Young teenagers undergo changes in their bodies to prepare them for reproduction. This is puberty.

After puberty girls release an egg on average every 28 days. This happens during the **menstrual cycle**:

Changes at puberty	
Girls	**Boys**
Hips get wider.	Shoulders get wider and voice deepens.
Breasts grow.	Penis and testes grow.
Menstruation (periods) starts.	Sperm is made.
Hair grows in armpits and around reproductive organs.	Hair grows on face, armpits and around reproductive organs.

After ovulation the lining of the uterus continues to thicken but if the egg is not fertilised the lining will start to break down.

Sometime around day 14 the egg is released from the ovary. This is ovulation.

The lining of the uterus breaks down and passes out of the vagina. This is a period.

After the period the lining of the uterus is repaired and an egg develops in the ovary.

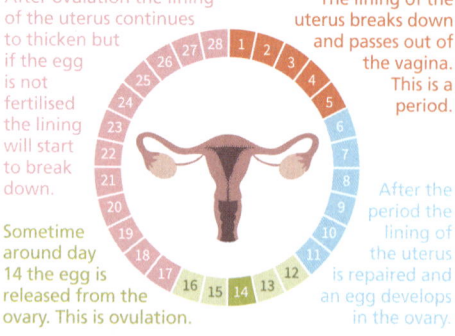

12

RETRIEVE 1: How does the human reproductive system function?

Female reproductive system

1 Write down the part of the female reproductive system that fits each description.

  a) The part where eggs are made ....

  b) The ring of muscle at the base of the uterus ....

  c) The tube that connects the uterus to the outside ....

2 Where in the female are eggs usually fertilised?

....

3 The oviducts can sometimes become blocked.

Explain why this may prevent a woman getting pregnant through sexual intercourse.

....

Male reproductive system

4 What is the name of the male sex cells?

....

5 Write down the role of these structures in reproduction.

  a) Testes ....

  b) Scrotal sac ....

Changes at puberty

6 What is puberty?

....

7 Give **one** change that happens to both girls and boys during puberty.

....

8 What is ovulation?

....

9 What is the average length of the menstrual cycle in days?

....

10 Sexual intercourse between about day 13 and 15 in the menstrual cycle often increases the chance of a woman getting pregnant. Explain why.

....

ORGANISE

1 How do humans reproduce?

Stages of pregnancy

Pregnancy is the time between fertilisation and birth. In humans, it takes about 38 weeks.

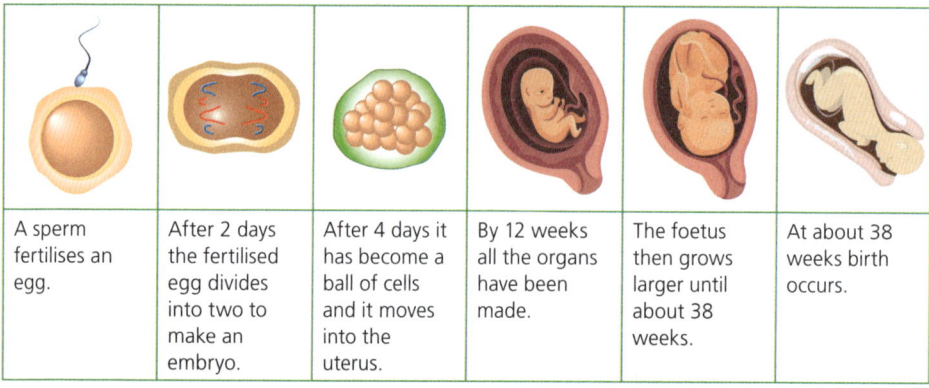

| A sperm fertilises an egg. | After 2 days the fertilised egg divides into two to make an embryo. | After 4 days it has become a ball of cells and it moves into the uterus. | By 12 weeks all the organs have been made. | The foetus then grows larger until about 38 weeks. | At about 38 weeks birth occurs. |

The millions of cells in a baby are produced from just one cell by cell division.

The uterus and the placenta

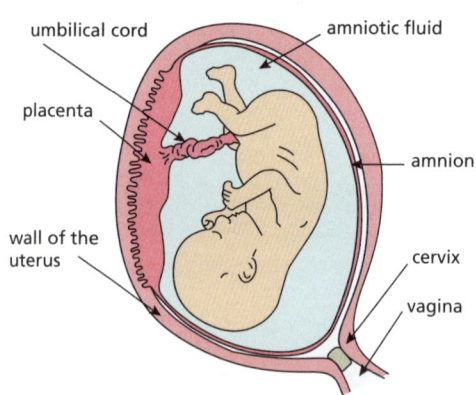

During pregnancy, the baby develops in the uterus. Different structures are important for the growth of the baby:
- the **placenta** allows substances to pass between the mother and the baby
- the **umbilical cord** contains blood vessels that connect the baby to the placenta
- the **amnion** is a membrane which surrounds the foetus and contains **amniotic fluid** to protect the baby
- the wall of the **uterus** has a lining which is attached to the placenta, and also has layers of muscle which are used to push the baby out through the vagina.

The placenta allows substances to pass between the mother's blood and the baby's blood:

From baby to mother	From mother to baby
Carbon dioxide	Oxygen
Waste materials such as urea	Food molecules such as glucose

In the placenta, the mother's blood and baby's blood do not mix; they are just very close together.

The placenta has different features to speed up the rate that substances can pass across:
- it has thousands of tiny finger-like structures to increase the surface area
- it has one layer of cells separating the mother's blood and the baby's blood
- it has many blood vessels to supply and remove blood.

RETRIEVE
1. How do humans reproduce?

Stages of pregnancy

1 How long is a typical pregnancy in humans? ....

2 Describe what has happened to a fertilised egg two days after fertilisation.

....

....

3 Describe the appearance of the embryo when it moves down into the uterus.

....

....

4 By 12 weeks a foetus has all its organs.

How does the foetus change between 12 weeks and 38 weeks?

....

The uterus and the placenta

5 Look at the diagram of a foetus in the uterus.

Write down the letter on the diagram that labels each of these structures.

a) The vagina ☐

b) Amniotic fluid ☐

c) The placenta ☐

6 How is the placenta connected to the foetus?

....

7 What is the function of the amniotic fluid?

....

8 The wall of the uterus is made of two different layers.

Describe the function of each of these layers.

a) An inner layer that contains many of the mother's blood vessels

....

....

b) An outer layer made of muscle

....

....

Biology 15

ORGANISE
1 What is a healthy diet?

Different food groups

Foods contain different nutrients. These nutrients fit into seven different food groups:

Food group	Example of nutrient	Function in the body	Good food source
Carbohydrates	Sugars, starch	Supply of energy	Fruit, milk (sugars) Rice (starch)
Protein	Casein (in milk)	Making cells for growth and repair	Milk, meat, fish, nuts
Lipids	Fats and oils	A store of energy	Milk, cheese
Minerals	Iron	Needed to make different cells and tissues	Spinach (iron) Milk (calcium)
Vitamins	Vitamin C	Needed to control different body processes	Oranges (vitamin C) Milk (vitamin D)
Fibre		Controls how fast food passes through the gut	Wholemeal bread, fruit
Water		Dissolves many substances in cells	

A balanced diet

It is necessary to eat the correct amount of each nutrient to have a **balanced diet**.

Food labels show how much of each nutrient is in the food. But different people need different amounts of each nutrient to have a balanced diet.

an athlete: 12 000kJ   an adult: 10 500kJ   a young boy: 10 500kJ

As well as nutrients, people also need the correct amount of energy (measured in kilojoules, kJ) in their food to have a balanced diet. Different people need different amounts according to their size and lifestyle.

Remember that a balanced diet is the correct amount of each nutrient. Do not write 'enough of each nutrient' as this could mean too much.

Food tests

Tests can be used to see if certain nutrients are in a food:

Nutrient tested for	Name of test	How the test is done	What colour can be seen if the result is positive
Sugar	Benedict's test	Heat with Benedict's reagent.	Orange-red
Starch	Iodine test	Add iodine solution.	Blue-black
Protein	Biuret test	Add biuret solution.	Purple
Lipid	Emulsion test	Add ethanol and then put a few drops into water.	Milky white

The test for sugar is the only test that needs heating and this should be done using a water bath.

RETRIEVE
1) What is a healthy diet?

Different food groups

1) What is the function of lipids in the body?

2) Name a good food source of starch in the diet.

3) Look at the table about food groups on the opposite page.

  a) Why is milk considered a useful food to have in a balanced diet?

  b) Why would drinking milk on its own not be a balanced diet?

A balanced diet

4) What is a balanced diet?

5) Look at the diagrams on the opposite page showing the energy needs of different males.

  a) How much more energy does an athlete need per day compared to a non-athlete?

  b) Why do athletes need more energy?

  c) A chocolate bar supplies 2000kJ of energy.
  What fraction of the athlete's daily energy need does it supply?

Food tests

6) What is the name of the test for lipids?

7) Describe how to test a food for sugar.

8) What colour is seen if biuret solution is added to protein?

Biology   17

ORGANISE

1) What is the human digestive system?

Structure of the digestive system

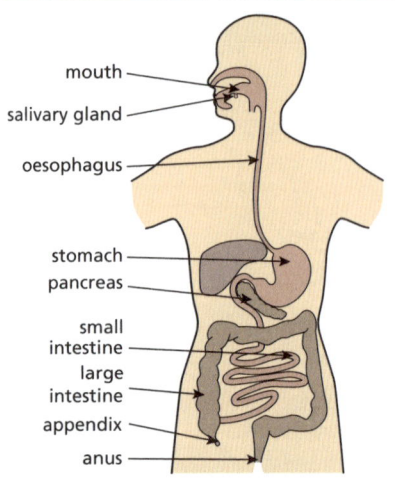

Labels: mouth, salivary gland, oesophagus, stomach, pancreas, small intestine, large intestine, appendix, anus

The human digestive system is made up of a long tube which passes from the **mouth** to the **anus**.
It also has several other organs which are attached to the tube:
- in the mouth there are connections to the **salivary glands**
- from the mouth, food passes down a long tube called the **oesophagus** (gullet)
- the oesophagus passes food into a muscular bag called the **stomach**
- after the stomach, there is a long, coiled tube called the **small intestine**
- the food then passes into the **large intestine**, which empties to the outside through the **anus**.

The small intestine is called 'small' because it is narrow. It is actually 9 metres long, which is much longer than the large intestine.

Digestion

Digestion involves breaking food molecules down into smaller, soluble molecules. This allows them to leave the digestive system and enter the bloodstream.

There are two types of digestion:
- **physical digestion** – caused by different parts of the digestive system churning or crushing the food
- **chemical digestion** – involves special protein molecules called enzymes that break down food molecules into smaller molecules.

Digestion of different nutrients takes place in different parts of the digestive system:

Part of the digestive system	Processes happening	How each part is adapted for its function
Mouth	• Food is physically digested by the chewing of the teeth. • An enzyme in saliva breaks down starch.	• The teeth and tongue chew and mix food.
Stomach	• The stomach contracts and churns the food. • An enzyme is released that breaks down proteins.	• The stomach wall has muscles that can contract.
Small intestine	• Enzymes from the pancreas break down lipids and any remaining starch or protein. • The digested food is absorbed into the bloodstream.	• It is connected to the pancreas. • It has thin walls and a good blood supply.
Large intestine	• Water is drawn out of the food into the blood.	

No digestion takes place in the large intestine but it is important for making semi-solid faeces.

18

RETRIEVE 1 What is the human digestive system?

Structure of the digestive system

1. Look at the diagram of the digestive system.

   Write the letters from the diagram that fit each of these descriptions.

   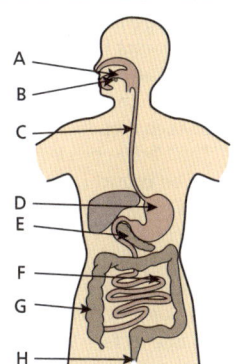

   a) The anus

   b) The pancreas

   c) A muscular bag

   d) The tube that connects the mouth to the stomach

2. Why is the small intestine called small, and the large intestine called large?

   ....

   ....

Digestion

3. Put **one** tick next to each statement to show if it is an example of physical or chemical digestion. The first one has been done for you.

	Physical digestion	Chemical digestion
Enzymes in the stomach digesting protein		✓
Starch being broken down by saliva		
Food being churned in the stomach		
Teeth chewing food		

4. Where in the digestive system are lipids digested?

   ....

5. Here are some of the parts of the digestive system.

   (Circle) any of the parts that make enzymes.

   | anus | large intestine | pancreas | salivary glands | stomach |

6. Why does the small intestine have thin walls?

   ....

   ....

7. Describe the function of the large intestine.

   ....

   ....

Biology 19

ORGANISE 1 — What is the human breathing system?

Organs of the human breathing system

Different parts of the breathing system have different functions:
- The **trachea** connects the lungs to the mouth. It has rings of cartilage to keep it open.
- The trachea divides into two tubes called **bronchi**, which in turn divide into many small **bronchioles**.
- The bronchioles end in millions of tiny air sacs called **alveoli**. Here gases pass in and out of the blood. The large number of alveoli provides a large surface area to speed up gas exchange. Their walls are very thin, so the gases do not have far to move in and out of the blood.

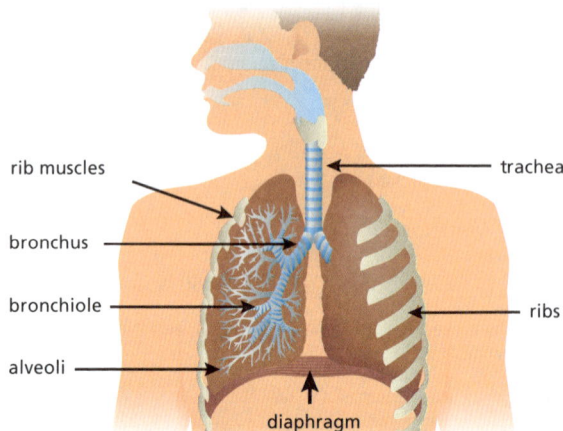

Breathing in and breathing out

- **Intercostal muscles** are found in-between the ribs.
- The ribs move up and out when the intercostal muscles contract.
- The sheet of muscle under the lungs is the **diaphragm**. This also contracts.
- Both muscle contractions cause air to be breathed in.
- When the intercostal muscles and the diaphragm relax, the ribs fall and air is breathed out.

Breathing is the process of moving air in and out of the lungs. This is **not** the same as respiration, which releases energy from food.

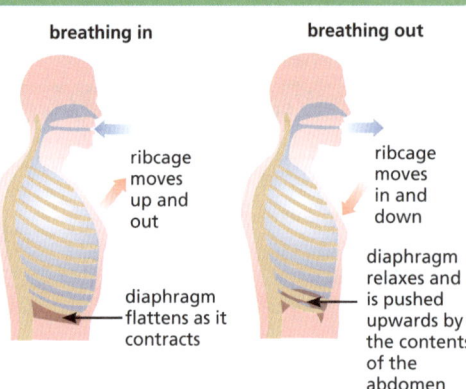

Asthma

When a person has an asthma attack, it is more difficult to draw air into and out of the lungs because the muscles in the bronchioles contract, which makes the tubes narrower. The bronchioles also contain more mucus.

Asthma may be made worse by:
- air pollution
- foreign substances, e.g. dust, pollen, pet hairs
- having certain genes
- breathing in cigarette smoke.

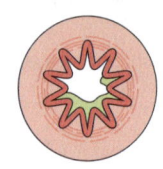

section through a bronchiole during an asthma attack

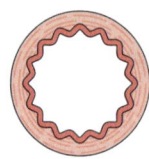

section through a healthy bronchiole

RETRIEVE

 # What is the human breathing system?

Organs of the human breathing system

1) Look at the diagram of the breathing system.

Write down the letter on the diagram that labels each of these structures.

a) A rib

b) The trachea

c) A bronchiole

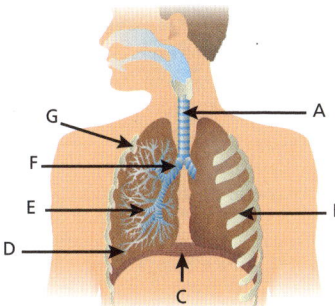

2) Why does the trachea have rings of cartilage?

3) Write down **one** feature of the alveoli that speeds up exchange of gases.

Breathing in and breathing out

4) Write these parts of the breathing system in the order that air moves through them when breathing in.

| bronchioles | trachea | bronchus | alveoli |

5) Name the **two** different muscles that contract during breathing in.

6) Explain the difference between breathing and respiration.

Asthma

7) Describes what happens when a person has an asthma attack.

8) Write **two** substances in the air that increase the risk of having an asthma attack.

Biology 21

ORGANISE

1 What is diffusion?

How does diffusion happen?

Particles in gases and liquids are always moving about.

If there is a difference in concentration then there will be an overall (net) movement from the area of high concentration to the area of low concentration. This is called **diffusion**.

Diffusion is faster if:
- it is warmer
- the concentration difference between the two areas is larger.

Diffusion is faster if it is warmer because the particles are moving faster.

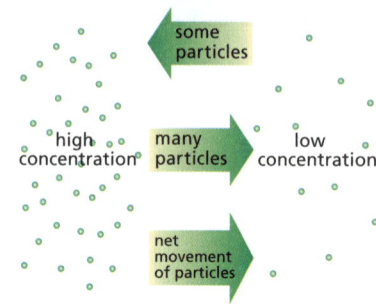

Diffusion in and out of cells

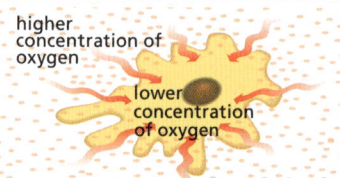

Cells take in and pass out substances across the cell membrane if there is a difference in concentration between the inside and outside. For example, oxygen is used up in respiration, so more will diffuse into the cell.

Other substances will diffuse into or out of the cell depending on the differences in concentration.

Diffusion will carry on until there is no difference in concentration between the inside and outside of the cell.

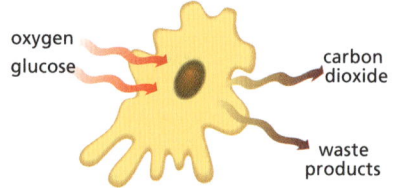

Diffusion in the body

Diffusion is very important for the movement of different substances in the body. Many of the organs in the body have these adaptations to speed up diffusion:
- a large surface area
- a rich blood supply
- a small distance for substances to diffuse.

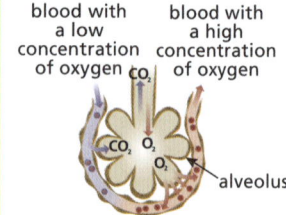	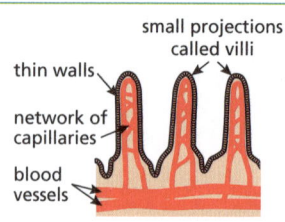	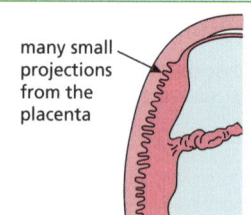
The **alveoli** (air sacs) in the lungs are adapted for diffusion of gases.	The lining of the **small intestine** is adapted for the diffusion of digested food molecules.	The **placenta** is adapted to allow substances to diffuse to and from the mother's blood.

RETRIEVE
 What is diffusion?

How does diffusion happen?

1 The diagram shows the molecules of a substance on both sides of a cell membrane.

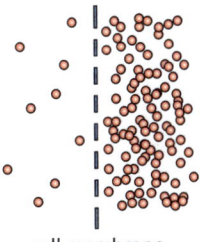

cell membrane

Draw an arrow on the diagram to show the direction of the overall diffusion of the molecules.

2 If the temperature was to increase, what would happen to the rate of diffusion?

3 Why does temperature affect the speed of diffusion?

Diffusion in and out of cells

4 Put a tick next to each substance to show if it normally moves in or moves out of body cells.

Substance	Diffuses in	Diffuses out
Oxygen		
Carbon dioxide		
Glucose		

5 Write the name of the process that uses oxygen in cells and makes carbon dioxide.

Diffusion in the body

6 Fill in the gaps to complete these sentences.

The tiny air sacs in the lungs are called ....

They are adapted to allow rapid diffusion of gases between the air and the ....

There are millions of air sacs in the lungs, which give a .... surface area for diffusion.

The air sacs have a .... lining, so that the gases do not have far to diffuse.

7 Explain why the lining of the small intestine has a large network of blood vessels.

Biology 23

ORGANISE
1 How can lifestyle affect disease?

Vitamin and mineral deficiency

Vitamins and **minerals** are:
- substances needed in very small amounts in the diet
- important for the correct functioning of the body.

Examples of vitamins are **vitamin C** and **vitamin D**.

An example of a mineral is **iron**.

Vitamin C	Needed for healing of wounds
Vitamin D	Strengthens bones
Iron	Used to make red blood cells

Lack of a vitamin or mineral in a person's diet can cause a **deficiency disease**.

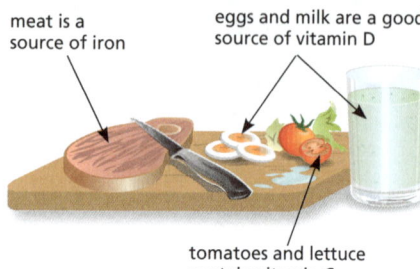

meat is a source of iron

eggs and milk are a good source of vitamin D

tomatoes and lettuce contain vitamin C

- **Lack of vitamin C** causes **scurvy**, which means that gums bleed and teeth fall out.
- **Lack of vitamin D** causes **rickets**, which can cause the bones to go soft and bend.
- **Lack of iron** causes **anaemia**, which is a shortage of red blood cells.

Obesity and malnutrition

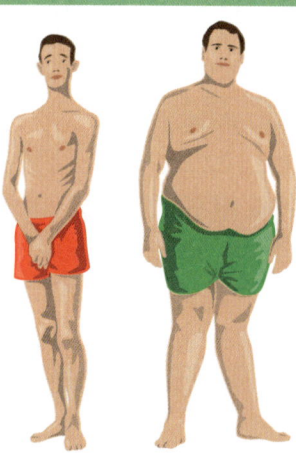

People have different amounts of body fat. **Obesity** refers to a person having too much body fat.

Obesity can increase the risk of:
- painful joints
- heart disease
- high blood pressure
- difficulties with breathing
- diabetes.

Obesity is caused by a person eating more food than they are using.

Starvation is caused by not eating enough food over a long period of time. This means that the person does not have enough nutrients for growth or energy. This can cause a decrease in muscle size and loss of hair. It can eventually lead to death.

Effects of smoking

Smoking cigarettes causes the body to take in different harmful chemicals, including:
- **nicotine**, which can increase blood pressure
- **carbon monoxide**, which reduces the amount of oxygen carried in the blood

- **tar**, which can damage small hairs in the lungs
- other chemicals, which can cause cancer.

If the small hairs in the lungs are damaged, mucus can build up and cause infections such as **bronchitis**.

Nicotine is an **addictive** chemical, which means that the body always wants more.

RETRIEVE

1. How can lifestyle affect disease?

Vitamin and mineral deficiency

1 Lack of which mineral or vitamin causes these deficiency diseases?

   a) Scurvy ....

   b) Anaemia ....

   c) Rickets ....

2 Choose a food from the list that is good for preventing each deficiency disease.

bread	eggs	lettuce	meat

   a) Scurvy ....

   b) Anaemia ....

   c) Rickets ....

Obesity and malnutrition

3 Obesity increases the risk of having certain diseases and conditions.

Name **three** of these diseases or conditions.

....

4 Explain why increasing exercise can reduce the chance of becoming obese.

....

5 Describe what happens to the muscles during starvation.

....

Effects of smoking

6 Smoking cigarettes is addictive.

What does addictive mean?

....

7 Which chemical in cigarette smoke is addictive?

....

8 Which chemicals in cigarette smoke can increase the risk of these problems?

   a) Bronchitis ....

   b) Increased blood pressure ....

9 What effect does carbon monoxide in cigarette smoke have on the blood?

....

Biology 25

ORGANISE

2 How do you work safely in a laboratory?

Hazard and risk

Hazards in a laboratory can come from **chemicals**, **glass equipment** and **hot objects**. The risk is the likelihood that the hazard will cause a problem like an injury. A **risk assessment** looks at how the risks can be reduced.

Personal protective equipment (PPE) should only be used if the risk can't be reduced any other way. If in doubt, always wear safety goggles to protect your eyes from chemical splashes, sparks or flying objects like splinters.

A lab has more dangers than a normal classroom. You should never be in a lab without a member of staff. Always follow your teacher's instructions while doing experiments.

Chemical hazards

explosive   flammable   oxidising

compressed gas   corrosive   toxic

irritant   environmentally damaging   health hazard

Hazard symbols **warn** of the dangers of substances even if a person can't read the writing on the container.

When working with a chemical, it is important that you:
- keep flammable materials away from naked flames and oxidising material to reduce the chance of a fire
- keep irritant, harmful and corrosive chemicals off your skin; wear gloves and eye protection
- use the smallest amount and lowest concentration of any substance.

Bunsen burners

Bunsen burners are used to **heat** things in labs. Use them safely by:
- only lighting the flame when the air hole is closed
- tying back long hair and tucking in loose clothing
- only using them while standing up
- putting the Bunsen burner in the middle of a flame-proof mat, away from the edge of a bench
- heating things while pointing them away from your face
- keeping the air hole closed when the Bunsen is not being used, so the cooler safety flame can be seen.

Rotating the collar lets more air into the Bunsen burner, which increases the temperature of the flame. When the air hole is fully open, the flame is blue and called the roaring or heating flame.

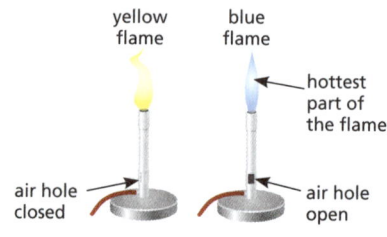

26

RETRIEVE
2) How do you work safely in a laboratory?

Hazard and risk

1 Draw lines to match the key terms to the correct definitions.

Risk		The dangers
Hazard		Evaluating the hazards and risks, giving ideas to reduce them and what to do if there is a problem
Risk assessment		How likely the dangers are to cause a problem

2 Name **one** piece of safety equipment that would help to protect you from chemicals splashing in your eyes.

....

Chemical hazards

3 Draw and name the hazard symbol that would be found on the side of a bottle of camping gas.

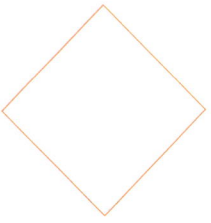

....

4 Name **two** pieces of safety equipment that would help to protect you from corrosive chemicals.

....

Bunsen burners

5 Explain how to get a safety flame on a Bunsen burner.

....
....

6 Suggest where the hottest part of a Bunsen flame is.

....

7 Explain why long hair should be tied back before you use a Bunsen burner.

....

ORGANISE
2. How do you record experiments?

Designing an investigation

Variables can be **changed** or **controlled**. In an investigation, you want to change one variable and observe the effect on another variable while keeping everything else the same. By collecting data in the investigation, you can find out if there is a relationship between the variables.

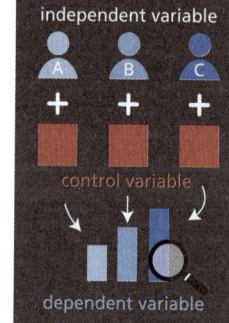

Independent variable	The variable you choose to change; always the first column in a results table (and the x-axis in a graph)
Dependent variable	The variable you are measuring in the experiment (always the y-axis in a graph)
Control variable	The variable that is kept the same to make a fair test and to collect valid results

The **method** is a step-by-step guide on how you will complete the investigation. It should be written in chronological order and include an equipment list.

> **Science** is the study of the physical and natural world through observations or surveys and experiments. It is important that you can plan investigations and communicate your ideas clearly.

Scientific drawings

Scientific drawings clearly show how **apparatus** is set up and used in an investigation.

Scientific drawings should:
- be drawn with a pencil and a ruler
- be at least half a page in size
- be 2D, not 3D
- be clear and unshaded
- have all equipment labelled.

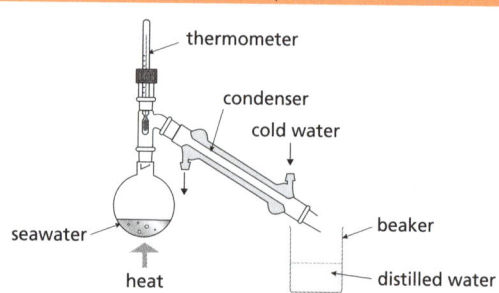

Results tables

In an investigation you are monitoring the dependent variable by using:
- your own senses and observing (e.g. noticing colour changes, fizzing or new smells)
- measuring instruments (e.g. a measuring cylinder).

Record your data as you collect it. Results tables record the information in an easy-to-understand way and you may start to see patterns.

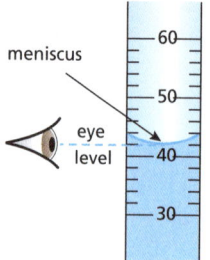

independent variable is always the first column

name and unit of the dependent variable in the column heading

Mass of powder (g)	Volume of gas (cm³)		
	First experiment	Repeated experiment	Average
1	5	7	6
10	90	95	92
5	27	23	25

as these values are chosen in the method, this column should be filled in before the investigation starts

data recorded to the same number of decimal places. Numbers only are needed in the main part of the table as the units are in the column heading

28

RETRIEVE

2. How do you record experiments?

Designing an investigation

1 Decide if the following statements are **true** or **false**.

Put a tick in the correct column to show your answer.

		True	False
a)	You choose to change control variables.		
b)	The dependent variable is on the *y*-axis.		
c)	The independent variable is always in the first column in a results table.		
d)	An investigation tries to find a relationship between the independent and dependent variables.		
e)	Dependent variables are the only type of variable that can be controlled.		

Scientific drawings

2 Add labels to show the apparatus in this scientific diagram.

3 Make a scientific drawing for the filtering of sand from water into a test tube.

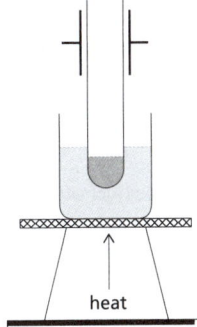

heat

Results tables

4 Explain why you can fill in the first column of the results table before you start your investigation.

_____

5 In the space below, draw a suitable results table for a student to measure the handspan of three triplets called Jan, Janna and Janine.

Chemistry   29

ORGANISE
2. How can you classify a substance?

Pure substances

Matter makes up everything. Matter is made of particles. If all the particles are the same, the substance is said to be **pure**. But often, a substance is made of different matter that is mixed together.

All matter is made of **atoms**. An atom is the smallest particle that can exist on its own. Some substances, like helium, are made of single atoms. But many single atoms, like oxygen, chemically join together to form **molecules**.

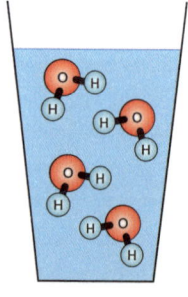

Scientifically, pure water contains only water particles.

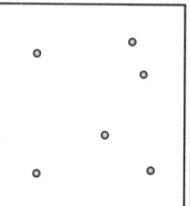

helium atoms (pure helium)

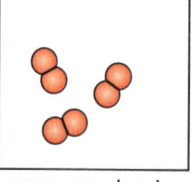

oxygen molecules (pure oxygen)

Elements and compounds

Elements contain only one type of atom and are listed on the **Periodic Table**. There are about 100 naturally occurring elements but they are difficult to find as pure samples, so many were not known until the 18th century and beyond. Every element has a symbol to represent it.

When more than one element combines, a **compound** is made. Compounds have different properties to the elements that they are made from. For example, carbon can join to oxygen to make molecules of carbon dioxide. The elements that make up a compound cannot be separated easily.

hydrogen atom, H

oxygen atom, O

Hydrogen and oxygen are examples of elements.

pure carbon dioxide gas

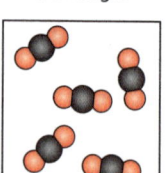

Molecules are more than one atom chemically joined together.
- If all the atoms are the same, then the molecule is an **element**, e.g. oxygen, O_2, hydrogen, H_2.
- If the atoms are different, then the molecule is a **compound**, e.g. water, H_2O, carbon dioxide, CO_2.

Mixtures

Mixtures are more than one type of substance not chemically joined.

Mixtures are never pure. Unlike compounds, they can be easily separated into the different substances that they are made of.

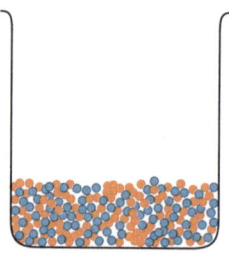

RETRIEVE
2) How can you classify a substance?

Pure substances

1 What is in a sample of pure oxygen?

2 Draw a diagram of pure hydrogen gas, H_2.

Elements and compounds

3 How many types of atoms are there in a sample of a pure element?

4 Where can you find a list of all the elements?

5 How many elements are there in a sample of a pure compound? Tick one answer.

Only one ☐

Two or more ☐

More than three ☐

6 Which elements are found in a molecule of carbon dioxide, CO_2?

Mixtures

7 Put a tick in the correct column to show whether the following statements are **true** or **false**.

	True	False
a) Mixtures are pure.		
b) Mixtures can easily be separated into the materials they are made from.		
c) Pure water is an example of a mixture.		
d) Salty water is an example of a mixture.		
e) Elements and compounds can be found in mixtures.		

Chemistry 31

ORGANISE
2) What is a solution?

Solutions

A solution is a type of mixture that looks like a transparent liquid. It is made up of two parts:
- **a solute** – the substance that is being dissolved; usually a solid
- **a solvent** – the main part of the mixture; usually the liquid.

Sugar can **dissolve** in water to make a sugar solution. Sugar is the solute and water is the solvent. The sugar particles separate from each other and fit into the gaps between the water molecules to form a **solution**. This means that the substances are **mixed** but no extra space is taken up, so the volume remains the same. This is an example of a **reversible change**.

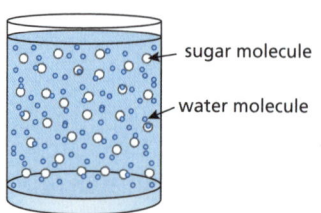
— sugar molecule
— water molecule

Making a **mixture** and separating a mixture are examples of **physical changes**. Physical changes are easily reversible and:
- there is no change in mass
- no new substances are made.

When a solution is made:
- mass of the solution
  = mass of solvent
  + mass of solute
- volume of the solution
  ≈ volume of the solvent

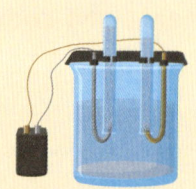

- Physical change: water boiling; no change in composition; easily reversible
- Chemical change: water electrolysis; new substances are formed; irreversible

Solubility

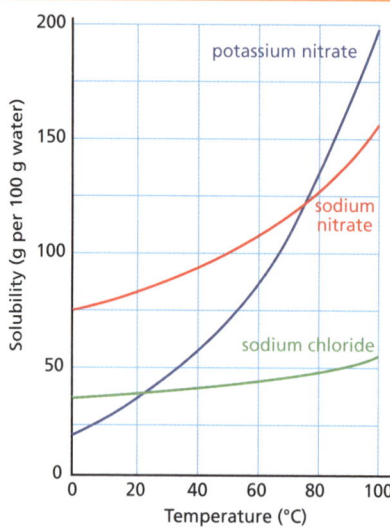

Solubility is the mass of solute that will dissolve in 100cm³ of a solvent at a given temperature.

A **solubility curve** is a graph that shows how solubility changes with temperature.

This graph shows three different solutes that have different solubilities.

Sometimes a substance will not make a solution and is described as **insoluble**. But by changing the solvent, a solution can be made.

Solubility is a measure of how much solute can dissolve into a volume of solvent at a precise temperature.

For solids, as temperature increases so does solubility. This means, at low temperatures, less solute can be dissolved into the same mass of solvent.

RETRIEVE
2. What is a solution?

Solutions

1) What happens to the mass of a substance when it undergoes a physical change?

2) Salt can be added to cooking water.

Tick the correct box to classify the parts of cooking water.

Substance	Solution	Solvent	Solute
Salt			
Water			
Salty water			

3) How do you know that a substance has dissolved?

4) Describe what happens when a solute dissolves.

5) What is the mass of a sugar solution made from 27g of water and 1g of sugar?

Solubility

6) How does solubility of a solid change with temperature?

7) What word would we use to describe a substance that will not dissolve?

8) Explain why solubility curves, where water is the solvent, are only given for a range of 0 → 100°C.

Chemistry 33

ORGANISE
2 How can you separate mixtures?

Separating mixtures

Mixtures can be separated by physical means. For example, a mixture of iron and sulfur can easily be separated using a magnet. The iron will be attracted to the magnet, leaving the yellow sulfur behind.

When choosing which **separation technique** to use, think about the properties of each part of the mixture:
- **Insoluble** – doesn't dissolve in that solvent, e.g. nail polish and water.
- **Immiscible** – doesn't mix, e.g. oil and water.

Techniques to separate mixtures

Separation technique and example	Separation technique and example

Sieving

e.g. Insoluble solid and a liquid, or two different sized solids

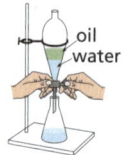

Gravel is collected in the sieve and the sand is collected below the sieve.

Chromatography

e.g. Inks and dyes

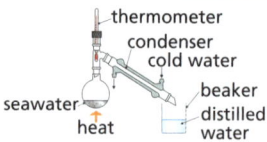

Coloured inks from a pen: The number of colours can be seen and the same ink identified from more than one sample.

Separating funnel

e.g. Immiscible liquids

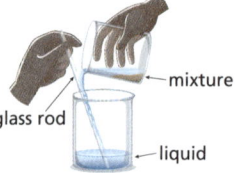

Oil/water: Water is collected, leaving oil in the separating funnel.

Distillation

e.g. Solvent from solutes in solutions

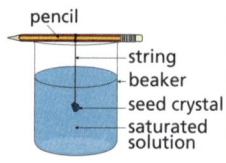

Tap water: Pure water is collected in the beaker and solutes are left in the round bottom flask.

Decanting

e.g. Insoluble solid from a liquid

Sandy water: Water is collected in a beaker, leaving sand behind.

Crystallisation

e.g. Solutes from solvents in solutions

Sugar water: Large sugar crystals form in a saturated sugar solution.

Filtering

e.g. Insoluble solid from a liquid

Sandy water: Sand is collected in the filter paper and the water in the test tube.

Evaporation

e.g. Solutes from solvents in solutions

Sugar water: Small sugar crystals are formed and the solvent (water) is lost to the atmosphere.

> Decanting and filtering both separate insoluble solids from liquids. Filtering gives a better separation than decanting as often some of the liquid remains in the solid as well as some of the solid transferring with the liquid.

RETRIEVE

2) How can you separate mixtures?

Separating mixtures

1 Fill in the blank to complete the sentence.

A mixture can be separated by .... means.

2 Draw lines to match the key terms to the correct definitions.

Insoluble		Dissolves in the solvent
Immiscible		Does not mix
Soluble		Does not dissolve in the solvent

Techniques to separate mixtures

3 Which separation technique can be used to separate immiscible liquids?

....

4 Which separation technique could you use to get pure drinking water from rainwater?

....

5 In the box below, draw a labelled diagram of the equipment that could be used to separate insoluble black charcoal powder from water.

6 Solutions can be separated using more than one method. Compare crystallisation, evaporation and distillation of salty water. Tick the correct box to classify each statement.

	Crystallisation	Evaporation	Distillation
Lose water to the atmosphere			
Collect pure water			
Collect large salt crystals			
Collect small salt crystals			

Chemistry 35

ORGANISE 2: How are separation techniques used in industry?

Salt

Salt that we use in cooking, and to preserve and flavour foods, is mainly a compound called **sodium chloride**, NaCl. Sodium chloride can be extracted from seawater or rock salt.

Sea salt

Seawater is a solution of many different types of salt including sodium chloride, calcium chloride, potassium chloride, and magnesium chloride. **Solar evaporation** is a technique where seawater is trapped in shallow ponds called **salt pans**. Over a day or two, the sun's energy evaporates the water, leaving the sea salt behind.

Rock salt

Rock salt:
- is a raw material found in the crust of the earth
- looks like brown, yellow or red rock
- is made from a mixture of sodium chloride and insoluble clay.

To **purify** rock salt, you can:
- grind the rock salt into small pieces
- add pure water and stir for a few minutes
- filter and collect the filtrate
- evaporate or crystallise the filtrate.

Solution mining is used to extract pure sodium chloride from rock salt. Water is pumped into a hole in the ground and the salt dissolves into the water to make **brine**. The water is then evaporated, leaving pure white salt crystals behind.

But the spaces left from solution mining can cause sink holes and destroy buildings.

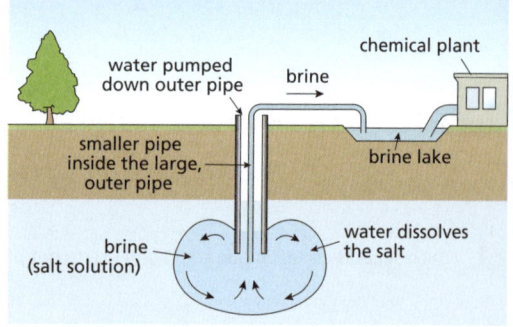

Rock salt can be mined and milled into small pieces for gritting the roads in winter. The sodium chloride lowers the melting point of the ice, so it melts and the insoluble clay gives grip to car tyres.

Distillation

Fractional distillation is used to separate a solution where there is more than one solute.

Each part of the mixture is called a fraction and will have a different **boiling point**. The equipment is similar to distillation, but a fractionating column is added to get a good separation of the fractions.

Fractional distillation can be used to:
- purify alcoholic drinks
- separate the gases in the air
- separate the different fuels in crude oil.

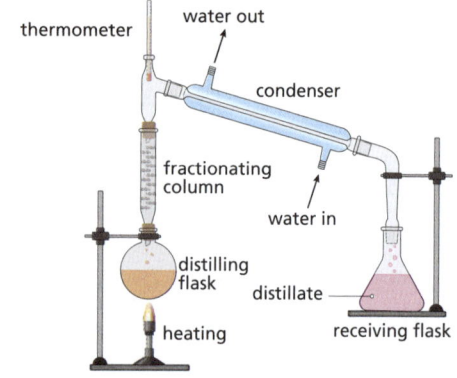

RETRIEVE 2: How are separation techniques used in industry?

Salt

1. What is the name of the substance NaCl?

Sea salt

2. Describe how a mixture of salts can be extracted from seawater on an industrial scale.

3. Put a tick in the correct column to show whether each of the following statements is **true** or **false**.

	True	False
a) Seawater is a solution of water with only sodium chloride dissolved in it.		
b) Solar crystallisation is used to extract salt from seawater.		
c) The energy to extract the salt from seawater comes from the sun.		

Rock salt

4. What colour is rock salt?

5. How is rock salt extracted from the Earth?

6. Give **one** use for rock salt.

7. Outline how pure sodium chloride can be extracted from rock salt in a school lab.

Distillation

8. What is fractional distillation used to separate?

9. Give **one** industrial use of fractional distillation.

Chemistry 37

ORGANISE

2 What is the Periodic Table?

Inventing the Periodic Table

In 1869, Dmitri Mendeleev was the first person to publish the **Periodic Table** of **Elements**. Only 64 elements had been discovered so he left gaps for new elements and made predictions about their properties.

The modern Periodic Table

Most elements are:
- metals and are found on the left and centre of the Periodic Table
- solids at room temperature.

Mercury (Hg) is the only liquid metal at room temperature and bromine (Br_2) is the only liquid non-metal at room temperature.

The elements that are gases at room temperature are all non-metals and are hydrogen (H_2), nitrogen (N_2), oxygen (O_2), fluorine (F_2), chlorine (Cl_2) and all the noble gases (helium (He), neon (Ne), argon (Ar), krypton (Kr), xenon (Xe), and radon (Rn)).

Since the first Periodic Table, technology has improved and new elements have been discovered. So, the modern Periodic Table has:
- no gaps
- Group 0
- man-made elements that are very heavy and unstable.

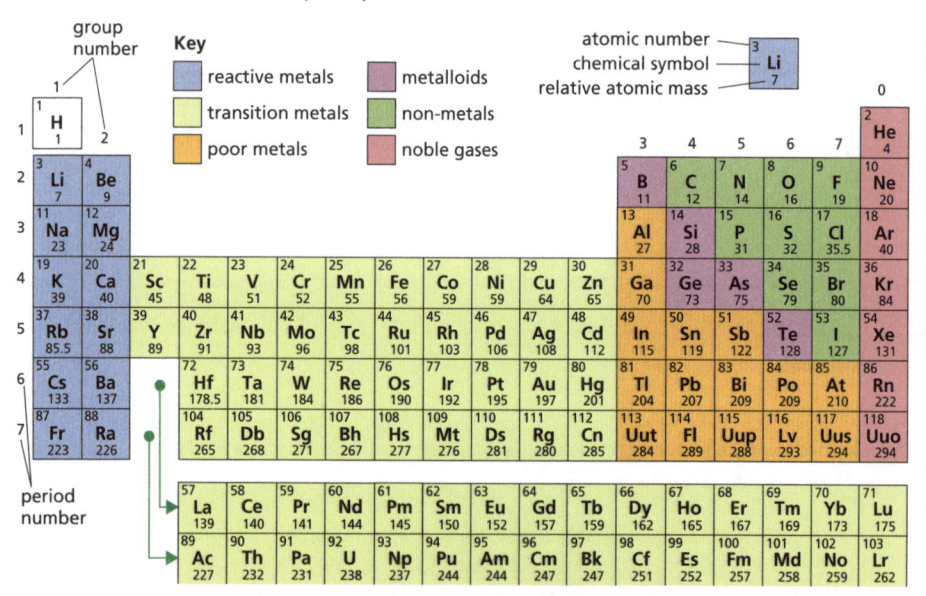

Finding information from the Periodic Table

All elements are listed on the Periodic Table. If we look at lithium, we can find out the following:
- its symbol is Li
- its atomic number is 3, meaning it is the third element in the Periodic Table
- its relative atomic mass is 7, meaning that the average mass of a lithium atom is 7 on the atomic scale. So, one lithium atom is 7 times heavier than one hydrogen atom.

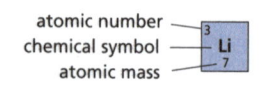

RETRIEVE 2 | What is the Periodic Table?

Inventing the Periodic Table

1 Who invented the Periodic Table?

The modern Periodic Table

2 What are the rows on the Periodic Table called?

3 What are the columns on the Periodic Table called?

4 Put a tick in the correct column to show whether each of the following statements is **true** or **false**.

		True	False
a)	Most elements are non-metals.		
b)	Metals are found on the left and centre of the Periodic Table.		
c)	There are two elements that are liquids at room temperature.		

Finding information from the Periodic Table

5 Look at the symbol tile for the element gold.

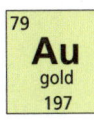

79
Au
gold
197

a) What is the symbol for gold?

b) What is the atomic number for gold?

c) What is the mass number for gold?

d) Which of these options completes the following sentence? Tick the correct answer.

Gold is a ....

metalloid ☐

transition metal ☐

Chemistry 39

ORGANISE
2. What are metals?

Metal properties

Pure metals are **elements** that are found on the left and centre of the **Periodic Table**. All metals have some properties in common:

Physical properties	Chemical properties
• Malleable (bend easily) • Ductile (can be made into wires) • Conductors (of heat and electricity) • Lustrous (shiny) • Sonorous (make a ringing sound when hit)	• Make basic oxides when reacted with oxygen

It is important to use the right metal for a job based on the metal's **properties**. Most metals that we use in everyday life are **transition metals**, e.g. copper, which is used for:
- cooking pans as it conducts heat, is malleable and does not react with food
- water pipes as it is malleable and does not rust or react with the water
- electrical wires as it conducts electricity and is ductile.

The **alkali metals** are found in Group 1 of the Periodic Table. They are:
- soft
- very reactive
- kept under oil or in airtight containers.

Metal extraction and alloys

Unreactive metals like gold (Au) are found as themselves in nature and are called **native** metals. But most metals are found in compounds called **minerals**. They are mined and the metal is extracted by a chemical reaction:
- **reduction with carbon** – used for zinc (Zn), iron (Fe), tin (Sn), lead (Pb) and copper (Cu)
- **electrolysis** – used for Group 1 metals, and aluminium electricity must be used.

Pure metals are often too soft to be useful. So they are mixed with other elements to make **alloys**. When iron is mixed with carbon, it makes a stronger alloy called **steel**.

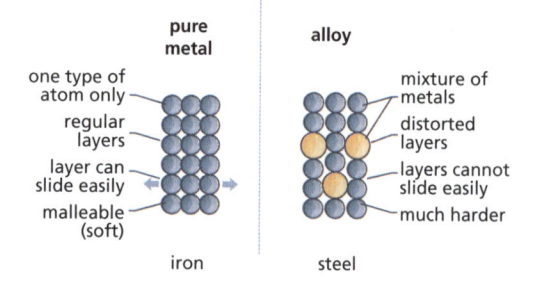

pure metal (iron): one type of atom only, regular layers, layer can slide easily, malleable (soft)

alloy (steel): mixture of metals, distorted layers, layers cannot slide easily, much harder

Iron and steel can rust. If chromium is added to steel, it makes an alloy called stainless steel, which is less likely to rust.

Flame colour

Some metal compounds can change the colour of a flame.

This is used to identify the metal and to add colour to fireworks.

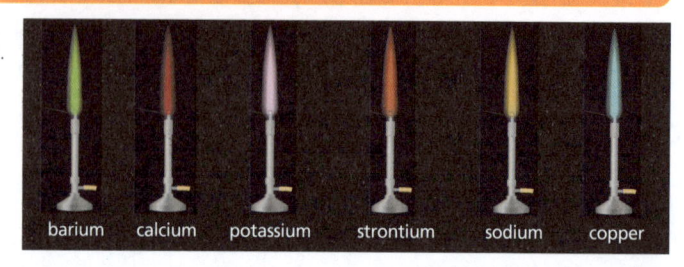

barium, calcium, potassium, strontium, sodium, copper

RETRIEVE

2) What are metals?

Metal properties

1 Which property of bronze metal makes it useful for making a bell?

....

2 Which property of gold makes it useful in computer electronics?

....

Metal extraction and alloys

3 Draw lines to match each metal to its method of extraction from the Earth's crust.

Gold, Au		Electrolysis
Aluminium, Al		Reduction with carbon, C
Iron, Fe		Mined as a native metal

4 What is an alloy?

....

5 What is the name of the alloy made of iron and carbon?

....

Flame colour

6 What colour would the flame be if a sodium compound was added?

....

7 Which metal would be present in each of these flames?

a)

b)

Chemistry 41

ORGANISE 2: What are non-metals and metalloids?

Non-metal properties and uses

Pure non-metals are elements that are found on the right of the **Periodic Table**. All non-metals have some properties in common:

Physical properties	Chemical properties
• Brittle (break easily) • Dull • Insulators	• Make acidic oxides when reacted with oxygen

Sulfur is a non-metal element that forms **allotropes**, where the atoms make different structures. Sulfur can be used to make rubber for car tyres, gunpowder and sulfuric acid. Humans also need about one gram of sulfur daily to keep healthy.

Carbon is a non-metal element in Group 4 of the Periodic Table. It forms two main allotropes:
- graphite – used in pencil lead as the layers of atoms can move and leave a mark
- diamond – used on drill bits as it is very hard with a high melting point, because the atoms are tightly locked into place.

Halogens are Group 7 elements. All of the halogen elements are hazardous but are still useful:
- chlorine is used as a disinfectant in pools
- iodine is an antiseptic and is needed in the human diet for a healthy thyroid gland
- halogen lamps contain bromine and iodine gas.

> Halogens form compounds with metals called salts. Fluoride salts are added to tap water and toothpaste to strengthen teeth, and chloride salts are added to food for taste.

Noble gases are Group 0 elements. All of the noble gas elements are **inert** colourless gases at room temperature.
- Helium is used in party balloons as it is less dense than air.
- Argon fills lightbulbs so the filament doesn't burn away.
- Neon is used in signs as it glows bright red when electricity is passed through it.

Metalloid properties

Pure non-metals are elements that are found on the right of the **Periodic Table**. All non-metals have some properties in common:

Physical properties	Chemical properties
• Semiconductors • Can form alloys with metals • Lustrous (shiny)	• Make oxides when they react with metals that can be acids and bases

We rely on the properties of metalloids to make faster and smaller electronics.

	Appearance	Thermal conductivity	Electrical conductivity	Density	Melting point	At room temperature
Metals	Shiny	Good conductors	Good conductors	High	High	Solids except mercury (liquid)
Non-metals	Dull	Poor conductors	Poor conductors	Low	Low	Solids or gases except bromine (liquid)
Metalloids	Shiny or dull	Semi-conductors	Semi-conductors	Fairly low	Between metals and non-metals	Solids

RETRIEVE 2: What are non-metals and metalloids?

Non-metal properties and uses

1 What type of substance is made when a non-metal reacts with oxygen?

2 Where are non-metals found on the Periodic Table?

3 Put a tick in the correct column to show whether each of the following statements is **true** or **false**.

	True	False
a) Sulfur is used in the manufacture of car tyres.		
b) Graphite and diamond are made from the same element.		
c) Graphite is an insulator.		
d) Fluorine gas is used to prevent tooth decay.		
e) Helium is used to fill party balloons as it is denser than air.		

4 What is an allotrope?

5 Give an example of an inert element that is a gas at room temperature.

Metalloid properties

6 Where are metalloids found on the Periodic Table?

7 What are metalloids used for?

8 Give **two** examples of metalloids.
Use the Periodic Table to help you.

Chemistry 43

ORGANISE 2: What happens to mass in a chemical or physical change (1)?

Chemical and physical changes

Burning is an example of a **chemical change**.
Chemical changes:
- are not easily reversible
- involve a new substance being made
- have no change in mass.

Melting is an example of a **physical change**.
Physical changes:
- are reversible
- involve no new substance being made
- have no change in mass.

Chemical changes of matter

nail → rusty nail

dough → baking bread

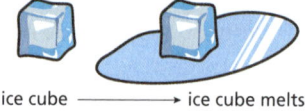

Physical changes of matter

butter → butter melts

ice cube → ice cube melts

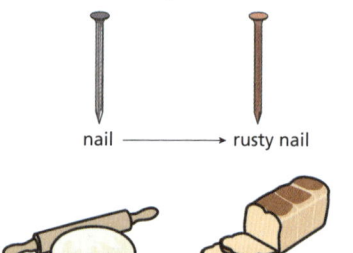

Observations that suggest a chemical change has happened include:
- bubbles or a new smell – this means a gas is being made
- a colour change – this suggests a new substance is being made
- a new solid is made
- a temperature change.

Conservation of mass

In a chemical reaction the atoms rearrange to make new substances. No atoms are lost or added, so the mass must remain the same throughout the chemical reaction.

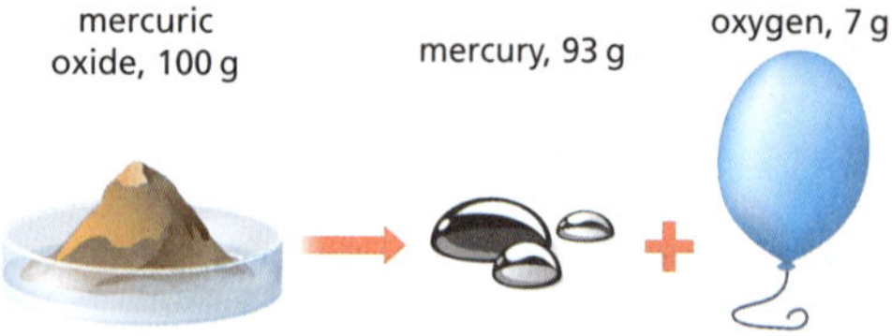

mercuric oxide, 100 g → mercury, 93 g + oxygen, 7 g

We can monitor the mass by using a **top pan balance**. We can see that the mass of the silver nitrate and sodium chloride at the start of the experiment is the same as the mass of the solution of sodium nitrate and the silver chloride precipitate made in the chemical reaction.

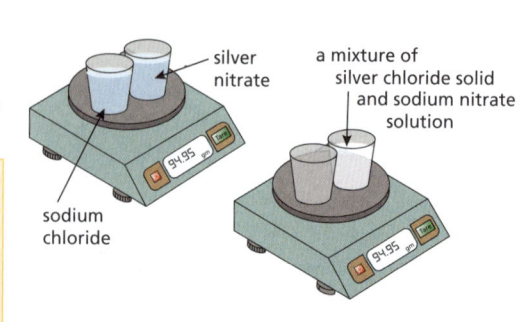

silver nitrate

sodium chloride

a mixture of silver chloride solid and sodium nitrate solution

> Sometimes it looks like the mass in a chemical reaction has changed. If bubbles of a gas are made and it escapes to the atmosphere, the mass will appear to drop. But if a substance reacts with gases in the atmosphere, then the mass will appear to increase.

RETRIEVE 2: What happens to mass in a chemical or physical change (1)?

Chemical and physical changes

1 Compare chemical and physical changes. Tick the correct box to classify each of the statements.

	Chemical change	Physical change
a) Mass does not change		
b) Easy to reverse		
c) A new substance is made		
d) Temperature change		

2 When you observe a chemical reaction, what do bubbles indicate?

Conservation of mass

3 What happens to the atoms in a chemical reaction?

4 10g of sodium hydroxide solution was added to 10g of hydrochloric acid solution.

What was the mass at the end of the chemical reaction?

5 40g of magnesium oxide was made from 24g of magnesium.

What was the mass of the oxygen used in this chemical reaction?

6 An iron nail had a mass of 0.4g. After a week, the nail had rusted and had a mass of 0.6g.

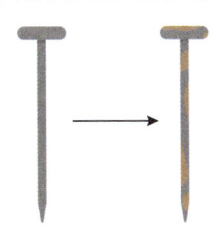

Explain the mass change.

Chemistry 45

ORGANISE
2. What happens in a chemical reaction?

Atoms in a chemical reaction

The starting substances in a **chemical reaction** are called the **reactants**. During a chemical reaction:
- the bonds between the atoms in the reactants break
- the atoms then rearrange and make new bonds to form the substances at the end of the chemical reaction.

The substances at the end of the chemical reaction are called the **products**.

Consider the reaction between hydrogen gas and oxygen gas to make water. When a flame is put to a balloon containing hydrogen gas, it explodes as a chemical reaction happens with the oxygen gas in the air. The product of this reaction is water.

We can use the **particle model** to describe what happens:

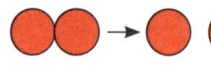

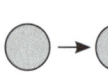

The reactants are two molecules of hydrogen and one molecule of oxygen.

The bonds in the reactants break to form two atoms of oxygen and four atoms of hydrogen.

The atoms re-arrange and make new bonds to form the products which are two molecules of water.

Word equations

We can summarise a chemical reaction in a **word equation**. Word equations give the names of the reactants and the names of the products that are formed in a chemical reaction.

Word equations should:
- include the names of all the chemicals involved in the reaction
- have an arrow (→) to show that the reactants go to the products
- have all the reactants written on the left side of the arrow
- have all the products written on the right side of the arrow.

> Never use an equals sign (=) in a chemical reaction: the reactants do not equal the products, they change into the products.

So, for the reaction between oxygen and hydrogen gas to make water, the word equation is:

hydrogen + oxygen → water

Symbol equations

Sometimes it is useful to imagine what happens to each individual atom in a chemical reaction. **Symbol equations** show the **formula** of each substance. As no atoms are created or destroyed, the symbol equation must be balanced. This means there are the same number and type of atoms on each side of the equation.

So, for the reaction between oxygen and hydrogen gas to make water, the symbol equation is:

$2H_2 + O_2 \rightarrow 2H_2O$

The large number in front of a formula shows that there is more than one of that substance. So in the equation above:
- **two** molecules of hydrogen, $2H_2$...
- react with **one** molecule of oxygen, O_2...
- to make **two** molecules of water, $2H_2O$.

RETRIEVE

2) What happens in a chemical reaction?

Atoms in a chemical reaction

1. What are reactants?

2. What are products?

3. In the box below, draw a particle model to show the chemical reaction between an atom of carbon and a molecule of oxygen to make one molecule of carbon dioxide.

Word equations

4. Write a word equation for the reaction between copper and oxygen to make copper oxide.

5. Write a word equation for the reaction to make copper oxide and carbon dioxide from copper carbonate.

Symbol equations

6. Sodium carbonate can react with hydrochloric acid. The symbol equation for this reaction is:

$$Na_2CO_3 + 2HCl \rightarrow 2NaCl + H_2O + CO_2$$

Put a tick in the correct column to show whether each of the following statements about this reaction is **true** or **false**.

	True	False
a) Na_2CO_3 is a reactant		
b) There are three different products made		
c) There are two HCl reactants for every one Na_2CO_3		
d) HCl is a product		
e) An → or = can be used in the symbol equation		

Chemistry 47

ORGANISE 2 — What happens in oxidation reactions?

Oxidation

Oxidation is a **chemical reaction** where oxygen is added to a substance. The general equation for a metal oxidising is:
metal + oxygen → metal oxide

Oxidation reactions can be:
- very fast, for example the oxidation of magnesium ribbon to make magnesium oxide
- slow, for example the oxidation of steel to make rust.

Oxidation of magnesium ribbon to make magnesium oxide

$2Mg(s) + O_2(g) \rightarrow 2MgO(s)$

It is oxidation reactions that make food go off. When fats react with oxygen in the air, we say they have gone rancid. Butter and cheese go hard, change colour and taste bitter as the fats slowly oxidise. Apples go brown and lettuce goes pink as they oxidise, which also changes the taste and reduces the shelf life.

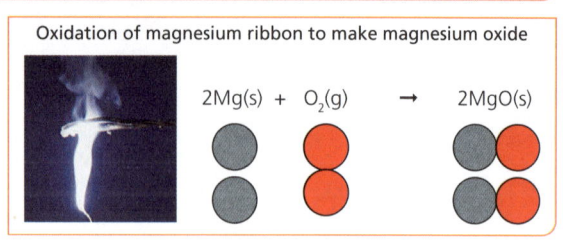

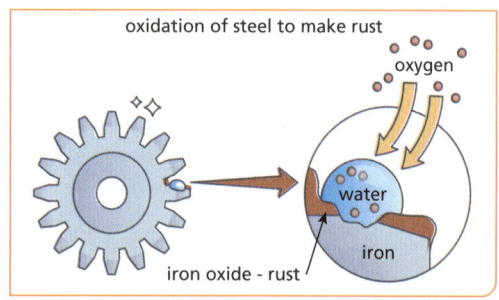

oxidation of steel to make rust
oxygen
water
iron
iron oxide - rust

Oxygen in the air

The amount of oxygen in dry air can be measured by oxidising copper using air. The mass of the copper oxide at the end of the experiment is compared to the mass of the copper at the start. From the data, we can calculate that air is made up of about one fifth oxygen.

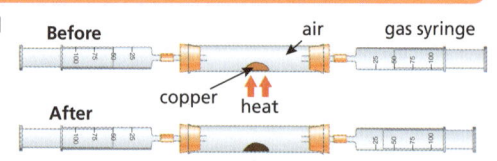

Before — air — gas syringe
After — copper — heat

Combustion

Burning is the everyday word for **combustion**.

Combustion:
- is a chemical reaction
- is a type of oxidation
- means stored chemical energy is transferred to thermal (heat) store and light
- always produces oxides.

Fuels like methane in natural gas are burnt in our homes to heat and cook. We can show this reaction in equations:

methane + oxygen → carbon dioxide + water

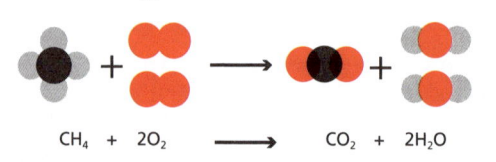

$CH_4 + 2O_2 \rightarrow CO_2 + 2H_2O$

oxygen is needed to burn

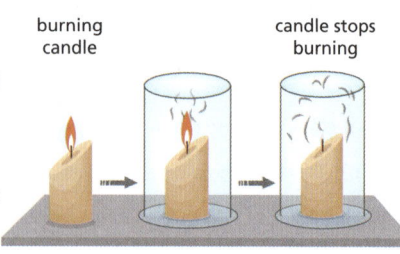

burning candle — candle stops burning
candle with jar full of oxygen — candle with lack of oxygen

48

RETRIEVE 2: What happens in oxidation reactions?

Oxidation

1) What is an oxidation reaction?

2) Write a word equation for the oxidation of magnesium.

Oxygen in the air

3) What percentage of dry air is oxygen?

4) Write a word equation for the oxidation of copper.

Combustion

5) Write a word equation for the combustion of ethanol to make carbon dioxide and water.

6) Tick the statements that are correct.

a) Burning is the same as combustion. ☐

b) Combustion is a type of chemical reaction. ☐

c) Oxygen is always needed for combustion. ☐

d) Oxygen is always a product of combustion. ☐

e) Combustion is an example of an oxidation reaction. ☐

7) What can methane be used for in houses?

8) What is always produced in a combustion reaction? Tick the correct answer.

nitrates ☐

sulfates ☐

oxides ☐

fuels ☐

Chemistry 49

ORGANISE 2: What happens in a decomposition reaction?

Decomposition

Decomposition reactions are **chemical reactions** as a new substance is made. The **reactant** is broken down into simpler substances.

A decomposition reaction can be:
- **electrolysis** – using electricity, for example, extracting aluminium metal from aluminium oxide
- **thermal** – using heat, for example, making calcium oxide from calcium carbonate, or using lime for making glass.

Metal carbonates

Metal carbonates are compounds made of a metal, carbon and oxygen.

Some metal carbonates can undergo **thermal decomposition** to make a metal oxide and carbon dioxide. The general equation is:

metal carbonate → metal oxide + carbon dioxide

Copper carbonate undergoes thermal decomposition. The word equation and symbol equation for this reaction are:

copper carbonate → copper oxide + carbon dioxide

$CuCO_3 \rightarrow CuO + CO_2$

There are some **observations** that show this is a chemical reaction:
- the solid changes colour from green to black
- a gas is made.

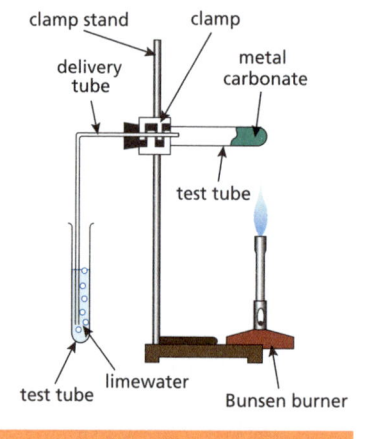

Limewater

Limewater is a solution of calcium hydroxide, $Ca(OH)_2$, which is colourless and turns cloudy as carbon dioxide reacts with it.

Limewater can be made by:
- thermal decomposition of calcium carbonate:
  – calcium carbonate → calcium oxide + carbon dioxide
  – $CaCO_3 \rightarrow CaO + CO_2$
- the chemical reaction between calcium oxide and water:
  – calcium oxide + water → calcium hydroxide
  – $CaO + H_2O \rightarrow Ca(OH)_2$
- a physical change as a solution of calcium hydroxide is made and collected as a filtrate.

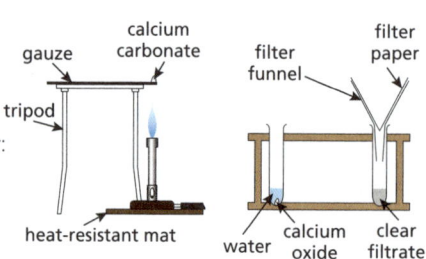

Limewater undergoes a neutralisation with carbon dioxide. Calcium hydroxide solution is an alkali and this reacts with the acidic carbon dioxide gas to make insoluble white calcium carbonate, which is why the solution looks cloudy.

calcium hydroxide + carbon dioxide → calcium carbonate + water
$Ca(OH)_2 + CO_2 \rightarrow CaCO_3 + H_2O$

RETRIEVE 2: What happens in a decomposition reaction?

Decomposition

1. Why are decomposition reactions examples of chemical changes?

2. What is used in thermal decomposition to break down the substance?

Metal carbonates

3. Which **two** non-metal elements are found in a metal carbonate?

4. Write a word equation for the thermal decomposition of lead carbonate.

Limewater

5. What is the chemical name for limewater?

    Tick the correct answer.

    calcium hydroxide solution ☐

    copper hydroxide solution ☐

    calcium carbonate ☐

    copper carbonate ☐

6. Draw lines to match the steps for making limewater to the type of change.

    | Heating the calcium carbonate |

    | Adding water to calcium oxide |

    | Adding water to solid calcium hydroxide to make a solution |

    | Filtering the mixture to collect the filtrate of calcium hydroxide |

    | Chemical change |

    | Physical change |

Chemistry 51

ORGANISE 2: What happens to mass in a chemical or physical change (2)?

Types of change

In science investigations, we observe changes and use them to draw conclusions. The changes can be classified as:
- a **chemical change**, e.g. **oxidation**, **burning** and **decomposition**
- a **physical change**, e.g. **melting**, **boiling**, making a solution or separating a mixture.

Mass

Mass is a measure of how much matter is in something. Mass is usually measured in grams, g, and is the same anywhere in the universe. In a chemical or physical change, the mass must stay the same.

Think about **dissolving** salt into water to make brine. The mass of the salt and water separately is the same as the mass of the brine made when they are mixed together.

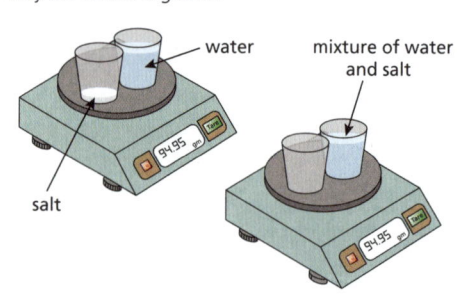

The Law of Conservation of Mass states that the mass of all the reactants must equal the mass of all the products. This is because in any change, no atoms are created or destroyed. For example:

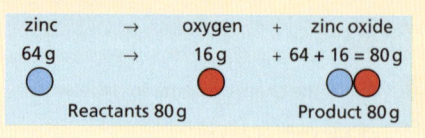

zinc → oxygen + zinc oxide
64 g   16 g   64 + 16 = 80 g
Reactants 80 g   Product 80 g

Oxidation: oxygen → zinc

But it is often changes that are happening in open containers which allow substances to be added or lost from the air and so it appears that the mass has changed:
- oxidation – oxygen is added from the air and so the mass looks like it has increased
- decomposition of a metal carbonate – carbon dioxide is lost to the air and so the mass looks like it has decreased.

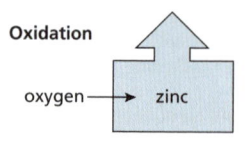

Thermal decomposition: copper carbonate → carbon dioxide

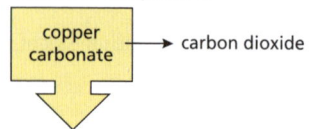

Density

Density is a measure of how much matter there is in a given amount of space. Density is usually measured in grams per cubic centimetre, g/cm^3.

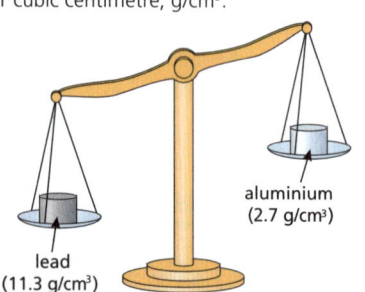

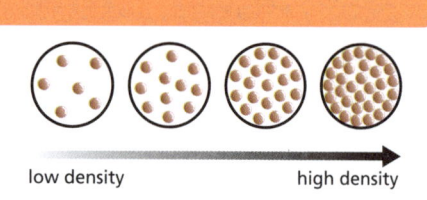

low density → high density

aluminium (2.7 g/cm^3)
lead (11.3 g/cm^3)

The equation to calculate density is:
density (g/cm^3) = mass (g) ÷ volume (cm^3)

If different metals are each made into blocks of the same size, the denser one would be heavier.

RETRIEVE 2: What happens to mass in a chemical or physical change (2)?

Types of change

1 What type of change is melting?

2 What type of change is oxidation?

Mass

3 What are the units of mass?

4 Put a tick in the correct column to show whether each of the following statements is **true** or **false**.

		True	False
a)	Mass appears to increase for decomposition reactions in open containers.		
b)	Mass appears to increase for oxidation reactions in open containers.		
c)	Mass of a solution is the same as the mass of the solute plus the mass of the solvent.		
d)	The Law of Conservation of Mass states that the mass of all the reactants equals the mass of all the products.		

5 Circle the correct words from the choices given to complete the sentences.

The Law of Conservation of Mass says that the mass of all the **reactants / elements** must equal the mass of all the **solutions / products** because **all / none** of the **elements / atoms** are created or destroyed in any change.

Density

6 What are the units of density?

7 What is the density of 105g of silver that has a volume of 10 cm^3?

Chemistry 53

ORGANISE 3: What is a force?

An introduction to forces

A **force** is a **push** or a **pull** that one object exerts on another object. For example, you might:
- push a car that has broken down
- pull a chair out from under a desk
- pull a door handle to close a door.

When a force is exerted on an object, it could make the object speed up, slow down, or change shape. For example:
- if you push on a shopping trolley, it will briefly speed up
- if you catch a ball thrown at you, it slows down to a stop
- if you pull both ends of a bungee, it increases in length.

A **newton-meter** can be used to measure the force needed to lift an object. Force is measured in **newtons**. The symbol for the newton is **N**. A force of about 1 N is needed to lift an apple.

The force needed to pull an object can also be measured using a newton-meter.

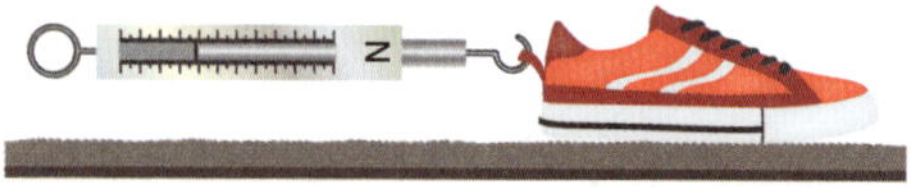

The stronger the force, the greater its value in newtons.

Force diagrams

A **force arrow** can be included on a diagram to show the direction of the force being exerted on the object.

In the diagram below, the bench is being pulled to the right. The red arrow pointing to the right represents this pulling force.

pull force

On a force diagram, a bigger force is represented by a longer arrow.

There may be several forces acting on an object. The child on the left is pushing the box with a force of 20N. The child on the right is pulling the box with a force of 15N. Both these forces can be shown on the force diagram. Notice that the smaller force is represented by a shorter arrow. Since both forces are directed to right, their effect would be to move the box to the right.

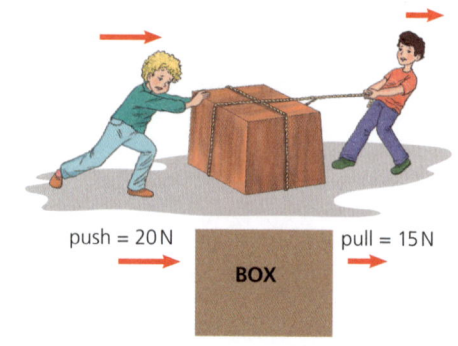

push = 20N   pull = 15N
BOX

RETRIEVE

3) What is a force?

An introduction to forces

1 Give an example of a push force acting on an object.

2 Give an example of a pull force acting on an object.

3 What are the **three** possible effects of applying a force to an object?

4 a) What is the name of the unit in which force is measured?
   b) What is the symbol for the unit in which force is measured?
   c) Give the name of the device used for measuring force.

Force diagrams

5 The direction of a force can be shown on a force diagram by an arrow.

How would the force arrow for a 10 N force be different to the force arrow for a 5 N force?

6 The horizontal forces on three stationary boxes, labelled A, B, and C, are shown as red arrows.

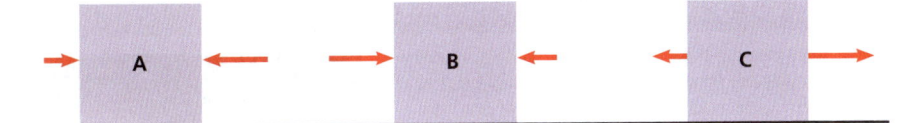

State in which direction, left or right, each box will move.

A:
B:
C:

7 Two children start to pull on a stationary trolley in opposite directions. The force diagram shows the two forces represented by arrows of equal length.

What is the overall effect of the forces acting on the trolley?

Physics 55

ORGANISE 3 — What is weight?

Mass and weight

- The **mass** of an object depends on how much matter is in it.
- Matter is made up of particles such as atoms and molecules.
- Mass is measured in **kilograms** (kg).
- Small masses are often measured in **grams** (g).
- The force of **gravity** is a pulling force that occurs between two masses. Like other forces, it is measured in newtons (N). However, the force of gravity is only big enough for us to notice if one of the two masses is a star or a moon or a planet, such as Earth.

> The force of gravity that a planet or a moon exerts on an object is called the object's weight.

In everyday life people often say 'weight' when they mean mass. But in science, since weight is the force of gravity on an object, it is measured in newtons.

> On the Earth, a mass of 1 kg experiences a force of gravity of 10 N. So a 1 kg mass has a weight of 10N.

A man standing on the Earth is being pulled towards the Earth's centre by the force of gravity. His mass is 70 kg so the force of gravity on him = 70 x 10 = 700N.

There is an upward contact force between the ground and his shoes. This force is also equal to 700N. These two forces cancel each other so the man remains stationary.

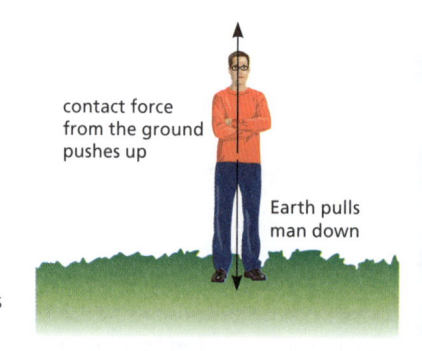

contact force from the ground pushes up

Earth pulls man down

Weight on other planets or moons

If you could travel to the Moon or other planets, would your mass and weight change? Your mass depends on how much matter makes up your body; if this does not change, your mass does not change.

Your weight depends on the force of gravity exerted on your body by the planet or moon you are on. Planets and moons vary in size so would exert different forces of gravity on you.

> Your weight depends on which planet or moon you are standing on.

The weight of an object depends on its mass and which planet it is located on.

The table shows the force of gravity exerted on a 1 kg mass on three different planets.

Planet	Mass in kg	Weight in N
Mars	1	3.7
Mercury	1	3.7
Venus	1	8.8

RETRIEVE 3 — What is weight?

Mass and weight

1 What does the mass of an object depend on?

....

....

2 Give the name of the unit used for mass measurements, and its symbol.

....

3 a) What is the alternative name for the force of gravity exerted on an object?

....

b) Give the name of the unit used for force of gravity measurements, and its symbol.

....

4 The diagram shows a box stationary on a table. There are two forces acting on the box. A force arrow has been drawn for one of the forces.

a) Name the force represented by the force arrow.

....

b) Give the name of the other force acting on the box.

....

c) Add a force arrow to the diagram to represent the force you have named in part b).

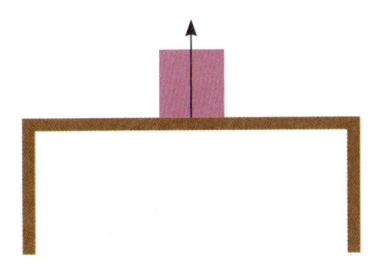

Weight on other planets or moons

5 An astronaut is to be transported from the Earth to the Moon. On the Earth her mass is 60 kg and her weight is 600 N.

a) Explain how the astronaut's mass and weight might be different on the Moon given that the Moon's gravity is weaker than the Earth's.

....

....

b) On which planet, Mars, Mercury, or Venus, would her weight be greatest? (Refer to the table at the bottom of page 56 to help you answer this question.)

....

Physics 57

ORGANISE
3 | How do forces interact?

Balanced and unbalanced forces

Forces can be balanced or unbalanced.

The diagram shows a brass mass suspended by a piece of string attached to a stand. There are two forces acting on the brass mass (shown by red force arrows). The upward force exerted by the string is equal in size to the downward pull of gravity. The two forces cancel each other so the mass is stationary. The two forces are described as being **balanced forces**.

> If an object is stationary, the forces on it are balanced.

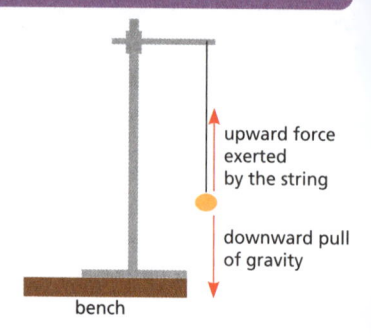

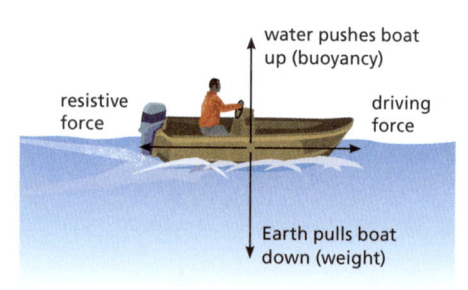

upward force exerted by the string

downward pull of gravity

bench

water pushes boat up (buoyancy)

resistive force

driving force

Earth pulls boat down (weight)

In this diagram, the boat is moving along a canal at a steady speed. The driving force on the boat is generated by the boat's engine. There is a drag force exerted by the water as the boat tries to move along the canal. The driving force and drag force are equal in size but act in opposite directions. They are described as being balanced forces.

> If an object is moving at a steady speed, the forces on it are balanced.

A tennis ball is approaching a tennis player. She hits the ball with her racquet. The force exerted by the racquet on the ball is not balanced by any other force. This **unbalanced force** slows the ball down, brings it to a stop, and then increases its speed in the opposite direction, back across the court. This all happens in a fraction of a second.

> The larger the unbalanced force exerted on an object, the greater its change in speed.

Action and reaction

If you catch a cricket ball moving fast towards you it is likely to hurt your hands. This is because when you exert a contact force on the ball to bring it to a stop, the ball exerts the same size contact force on your hands.

The force you exert on the ball is called the **action**. The force the ball exerts back on your hands is called the **reaction**.

> Action and reaction forces are the same type of force and the same size, but act in opposite directions.

RETRIEVE
3) How do forces interact?

Balanced and unbalanced forces

1 As the cyclist is pedalling, he travels at a steady speed along a flat road.

  a) The road is exerting an upward contact force on the bicycle wheels. Describe the force acting on the cyclist that is the same size but acting in the opposite direction to the upward contact force.

  ....

  b) The cyclist's pedalling generates a horizontal driving force in the forward direction. There is a drag force acting on him in the reverse direction. The drag force is caused by the air and by the contact between the tyres and the road.

  The cyclist is travelling at a steady speed so the horizontal forces on him and his bicycle are balanced. What does this tell you about the size and direction of the driving force and the drag force?

  ....

2 When a skydiver first jumps from the aircraft, she falls faster and faster. Her speed is increasing because the vertical forces acting on her are not balanced.

  a) The two vertical forces acting on the skydiver are her weight and an upward drag force caused by the air. Which of these two forces is the largest? Explain your answer.

  ....

  ....

  b) The drag force acting on the skydiver gets bigger as her speed increases. After falling for 10s her speed stops increasing and becomes steady. After falling for 10s, are the drag force and her weight balanced or unbalanced forces?

  ....

Action and reaction

3 A car crashed into a wall. When the car crashed, it exerted a 500N contact force on the wall.

Describe the force that the wall exerts on the car. Include its type, its size and its direction.

....

....

Physics 59

ORGANISE 3: What happens when a force is applied to elastic materials?

Forces causing a change of shape

As well as causing changes in motion, forces can also cause a change of shape. Squashing, stretching or bending, or a combination of these, can cause an object to change shape. For example:

| squashing a drinks can by hand | stretching a fitness stretch band | bending a long bow |

When a force deforms an object, the change in shape may be permanent, as in the case of the drinks can.

However, the deformation of the stretch band and the long bow is only temporary. They return to their original shape when the force is removed.

> Objects that return to their original shape after being deformed are made of **elastic** material.

Rubber is an elastic material so it can be used to make a catapult:
- The original length of the rubber band on the catapult is 18 cm.
- When stretched, the rubber band is 28 cm long.
- The rubber band's increase in length = 28 – 18 = 10 cm.
  This increase in length is also known as the **extension**.

> extension = stretched length – original length

A neck pillow made of polyurethane foam can be used by a passenger in a car to provide comfort during a long journey:
- Polyurethane foam is an elastic material.
- Your head, resting on the pillow, may cause a **compression** of about 1 cm, but the pillow returns to its original shape after use.

> compression = original thickness – compressed thickness

Hooke's Law

The extension of some elastic materials doubles when the stretching force applied is doubled.

These materials are said to obey **Hooke's Law**.

A coil spring, which has not been over-stretched, obeys Hooke's Law. The extension of the spring can be measured for different stretching forces and a graph plotted. The graph is a straight line which passes through (0,0). This point is called the **origin**.

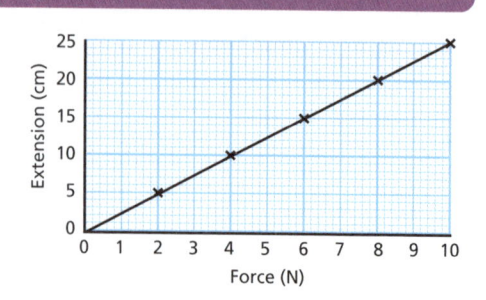

> If the extension against force graph for a material is a straight line that passes through the origin, then the material obeys Hooke's Law.

RETRIEVE 3: What happens when a force is applied to elastic materials?

Forces causing a change of shape

1 A force can change the shape of an object by causing it to be stretched. Name **two** other ways that the shape of an object can be changed by a force.

....

2 A spring is suspended from a clamp. Describe how to measure the extension of the spring caused by attaching the mass.

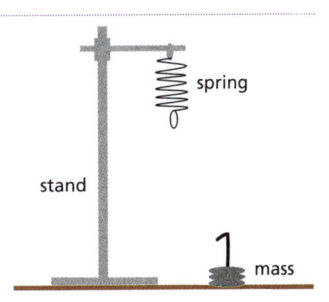

....

....

....

3 Three masses are used to compress a spring. Describe how to measure the compression of the spring.

....

....

....

Hooke's Law

4 Describe how stretching force and extension are related for a material that obeys Hooke's Law.

....

5 The sketch graphs of extension against stretching force for three materials, labelled A, B, and C, are shown below.

a) Tick the correct graph to show which material obeys Hooke's Law.

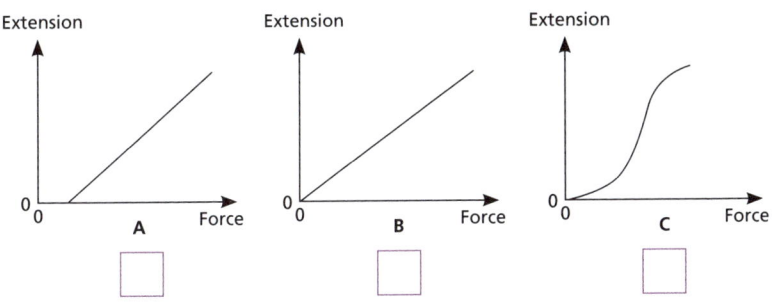

b) Explain your answer to part a).

....

....

Physics 61

ORGANISE

3 What is friction?

What causes friction?

When two solid objects touch, the molecules in both surfaces are in very close contact. Molecules close to other molecules attract each other. Also, surfaces are not perfectly smooth; there are tiny ridges and hollows. Surface roughness and molecule attraction resists the motion of one object sliding across the other. This resistance is called **friction**.

Friction can be useful. Examples include:
- the friction between paper and the tip of a pen helps with writing
- the friction between the soles of your shoes and the ground stops your feet slipping
- overcoming friction when rubbing your hands together generates thermal energy which warms them on a cold day.

> The resistance to the movement of one surface across another surface is due to friction.

Frictional forces occur when objects move through liquids and gases.
- When you are swimming in a pool, the water opposes your motion. This effect is **water resistance**. Your swimming action pushes the water aside so you can move forward.
- When you are walking, the opposition of the air to your motion is not noticeable but if you are moving faster, for example, on a bike, the opposition of the air to your motion increases. This effect is **air resistance**. When going fast downhill in a cycle race, cyclists take up a streamlined body position to reduce air resistance and go faster.

Changing friction

If water is spilt on smooth flooring it reduces friction, making it likely that people will slip. Similarly, wet grass can be slippery. A good grip on the sole of a shoe can increase friction and prevent slipping.

Water, ice or snow on the road can reduce friction between car tyres and the road surface. It is important that cars have good quality tyres so there is enough friction to prevent skidding.

Engines, and other types of machines, contain moving metal parts. Friction between moving parts can cause damage. Adding a **lubricant** can reduce this friction.

For example, synthetic oil can be used as a lubricant on a bicycle chain and chainring to keep them running smoothly.

> In reducing friction, oil is acting as a lubricant.

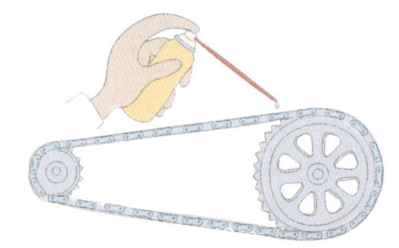

62

RETRIEVE 3: What is friction?

What causes friction?

1 Describe a cause of friction when one solid object moves across the surface of another solid object.

2 Give the name of the frictional force that opposes the motion of a barge as it travels along a canal.

3 Give the name of the frictional force that opposes the motion of an aircraft in flight.

4 The cyclist and her bicycle are affected by friction as she cycles along the road.

For each example, tick the correct column to say whether the effect of friction is **useful** or **not useful** to the cyclist. Then explain your choice.

Example	Useful	Not useful	Explanation
a) Friction between the soles of the cyclist's shoes and the pedals.			
b) Air resistance acting on the cyclist and her bicycle.			
c) Friction between the bicycle chain and chainring.			
d) Friction between the cyclist's hands and the handlebars.			

Changing friction

5 How is a boat designed to reduce the water resistance acting on its surface as it moves through the water?

6 Friction between the soles of your shoes and the footpath helps to stop you from slipping. What feature of your shoes increases this friction?

7 Name a lubricant that is used to reduce friction between moving parts in an engine.

8 In the UK, car tyres must have a tread that is at least 1.6 mm in depth. Suggest why this is the case.

Physics 63

ORGANISE 3: How do forces affect speed and direction?

Forces causing changes of speed and direction

On the Moon there is no atmosphere. So, if a hammer is dropped on the Moon, there is no air resistance force acting on it. The only force on the hammer is the force of gravity, which increases the speed of the hammer as it falls.

The diagram shows a satellite moving at a steady speed in its orbit around the Earth. The satellite is above the Earth's atmosphere so there is no air resistance force acting on it. The only force acting on the satellite is the force of gravity exerted by the Earth. This force always points towards the centre of the Earth. The force of gravity keeps changing the direction of the satellite so that it follows a circular path.

A force can change:
- the speed of an object
- an object's direction.

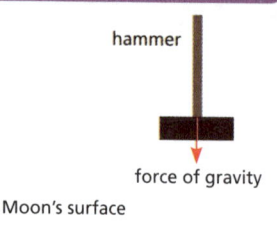

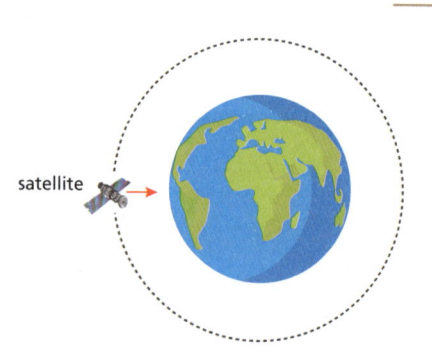

Controlling forces to create changes in speed and direction

This vehicle is being driven in the direction of the dotted arrow along a flat, curved track. When the driver turns the steering wheel, a force of friction is created between the road and the tyres. The friction force enables the car to follow the curved track. The driver must carefully control the steering wheel and the car's speed to get just the right amount of friction.

The football is approaching the football player and she is preparing to kick the ball. She applies a contact force to the ball with her foot. The force she applies must change the ball's direction and speed by a precise amount.

If she judges the size and direction of the contact force correctly, she may well score a goal.

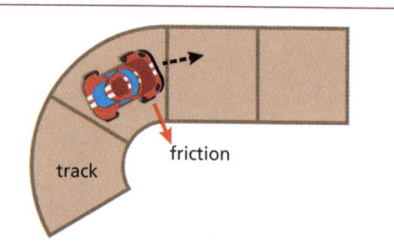

Precise control of the size and direction of a force can change an object's speed and direction exactly as is required.

RETRIEVE 3 — # How do forces affect speed and direction?

Forces causing changes of speed and direction

1 A piece of stone falls from the top of a tower. There are two forces acting on the stone. The force arrows are labelled X and Y on the diagram. The sizes of the forces are shown by the length of the arrows.

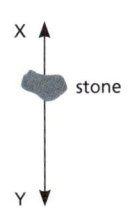

a) Give the names of the two forces.

X: ....

Y: ....

b) At the instant shown in the diagram, which force, X or Y, is the largest?

....

c) At the instant shown in the diagram, is the stone speeding up or falling at a steady speed? Explain your answer.

....

d) If someone had thrown the same piece of stone from the top of a tower it would follow the path shown by the dotted line. There are still two forces, X and Y, acting on the stone.

Does the direction of X or Y change, as the stone follows the path shown?

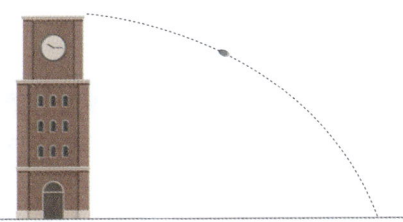

X: ....

Y: ....

Controlling forces to create changes in speed and direction

2 A boy is playing a game of darts.

The diagram shows a side view of the dartboard. The boy stands a few metres from the dart board. He throws the dart in the direction shown by the dotted line, straight at the centre of the dartboard.

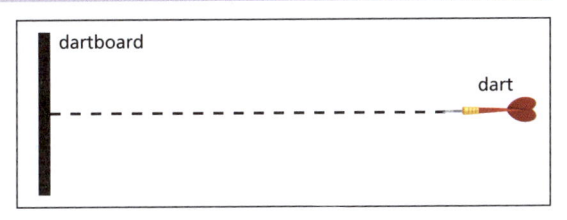

a) Add a force arrow to the diagram to show gravity acting on the arrow.

b) Will the dart hit the centre of the board? Explain your answer.

....

....

Physics 65

ORGANISE 3: What is speed?

Measuring speed

Speed is a measure of how fast an object is moving. The speed of a car is shown by the **speedometer** on the car's dashboard.

The speedometer gives the car's **actual speed** at the instant the driver looks at the speedometer. During any journey, a car's speed changes. For example, the driver will have to slow down when approaching roundabouts and stop at traffic lights.

The speedometer gives the car's speed as 55 miles per hour, which means that if the car continued at this speed, after one hour, the car would have travelled 55 miles.

This speedometer gives a car's speed in units of miles per hour (mph). Some speedometers also give speed in kilometres per hour (km/h). A speed of 88 km/h is the same as 55 mph.

The diagram shows a model train travelling around its track at a constant speed of 20 cm per second. This means that as each second passes, the model train has travelled another 20 cm. The speed of the train can be written as 20 cm/s.

Units for speed include miles per hour, kilometres per hour, metres per second and centimetres per second.

Calculating speed

Speed can be calculated using the equation shown.

For example:
- A student walks a short distance of 300 m to her school. The time taken to walk this distance is 5 minutes.

speed = distance ÷ time

First, we shall convert 5 minutes to seconds:
- There are 60 seconds in 1 minute, so 5 minutes = 5 × 60 = 300 seconds
- The student's speed = distance ÷ time = 300 ÷ 300 = **1 m/s**.

This value is her **average speed**. Her actual speed at different points in her journey may be a little faster or slower.

An athlete is running a 100 m race. The race is videoed so his actual speed at different points in the race can be measured. The athlete completes the race in 10 seconds:
- his average speed = distance ÷ time = 100 ÷ 10 = 10 m/s
- his actual speed, 2 seconds from the start, is 8 m/s
- his actual speed, 8 seconds from the start, is 11 m/s.

Actual speed has different values during a race or journey. Average speed applies to the whole race or journey.

RETRIEVE

3) What is speed?

Measuring speed

1 The image shows a car's speedometer in kilometres per hour.

　a) What is the car's speed at the point in the journey when the photo is taken? Tick the correct option.

　　80 km/h ☐

　　90 km/h ☐

　　100 km/h ☐

　b) Is your answer to part a) the car's average speed or the actual speed?

　　...

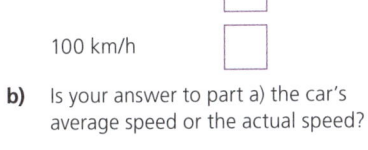

2 A cyclist travels for 1 hour at an average speed of 22 km/h. She continues for another hour at the same average speed. What is the total distance travelled? .... km

3 A person is walking for half an hour at an average speed of 4 miles per hour. What distance does the person walk? .... miles

4 A remote control toy car has a steady speed of 50 cm/s. How far does the car move in 2 seconds? .... cm

Calculating speed

5 An athlete completes a 200 metre race in 20 seconds.

Use the following equation to calculate the athlete's average speed in metres per second:

speed = distance ÷ time .... m/s

6 A train travels 200 km in 4 hours. Calculate the train's average speed in km/h. .... km/h

7 A cyclist travels along a straight road of length 1.8 km.

　a) Convert 1.8 km to metres by multiplying by 1000. .... m

　b) The cyclist travels the length of the road in 5 minutes. Convert 5 minutes to seconds by multiplying by 60. .... s

　c) Use your answers to parts a) and b) to calculate the cyclist's average speed in m/s. .... m/s

8 Explain the difference between average speed and actual speed.

....

....

Physics 67

ORGANISE 3 — What is a lever?

The main parts of a lever

A **lever** is made up of a solid beam (or bar or rod), and a **fulcrum** (or pivot), a point that the beam can **pivot** around. At some point on the beam, a person applies a force. This is called the **effort**. At another point on the beam is the object to be moved. This is called the **load**.

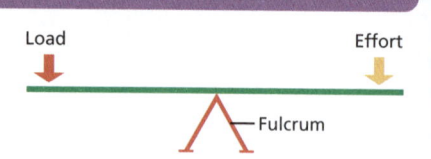

Creating a turning force with a lever

The man wants to move the boulder. But the force he can create with just his own body is not big enough so he uses a long metal rod as a lever and a smaller stone as a fulcrum. He exerts a force (effort) on the rod as far from the fulcrum as possible. The rod pivots around the fulcrum and exerts a turning force on the boulder. This **turning force** is big enough to move the boulder.

> The turning force generated by a lever is much larger than the effort if the load is much closer to the fulcrum than the effort.

A spanner can be used to tighten a nut on a bolt. The spanner acts as the lever. The bolt acts as the fulcrum and the nut is the load. Applying the effort force at one end of the spanner creates a turning force at the other end, which is much larger than the effort force and can rotate the nut so it is very tight on the bolt. The effort force turns the spanner in a clockwise direction.

> The effort force has to be moved through a much greater distance than the load moves.

A heavy load of soil can be moved in a wheelbarrow. The wheelbarrow acts like a lever. The axle through the middle of the wheel acts as the fulcrum. The gardener exerts a lifting force (effort) on the handles. This creates a turning force which rotates the wheelbarrow in a clockwise direction, lifting the load. This turning force is much greater than the effort force exerted by the gardener.

> An effort force turns a lever clockwise or anticlockwise.

In each of the examples above, the lever enables a much greater turning force to be applied to a load than the person could do with their bare hands.

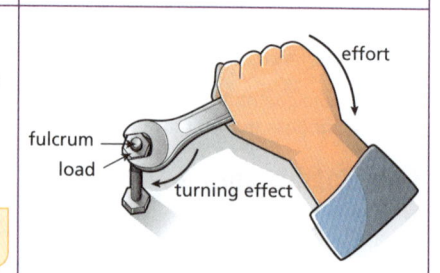

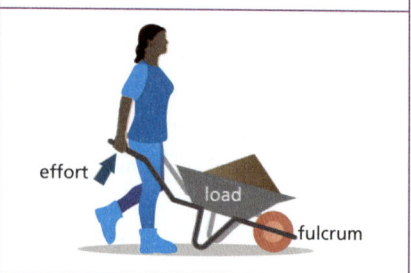

> The size of the turning force exerted on a load can be increased if:
> - the distance from the effort force to the fulcrum is increased
> - the distance from the load to the fulcrum is decreased
> - the size of the effort force is increased.

RETRIEVE

3 What is a lever?

The main parts of a lever

1 The diagram shows a wooden beam acting as a lever.

The lever is to be used to move a boulder labelled 'load'.

a) Add an **X** to the diagram to identify the fulcrum.

b) What is the alternative name for a fulcrum?

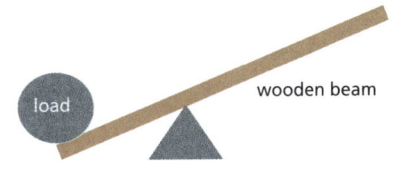

....

c) Add an arrow to the diagram to show the direction of the effort force.

Creating a turning force with a lever

2 The hammer has a claw end and is being used as a lever. A carpenter applies the effort force to remove a nail that is stuck in a piece of wood.

a) Label an **X** on the diagram to show the point that is acting as the fulcrum.

b) Which moves through the greater distance, the effort or the load?

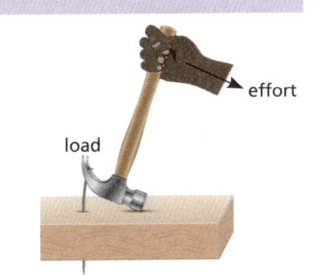

....

3 A spanner is being used as a lever to remove a nut that is very tight on a rusty bolt. The arrow shows the direction of the effort force applied by the person's hand. The bolt is acting as the fulcrum.

a) Applying the effort force to the end of the spanner creates a large turning force which loosens the nut. Is this turning force rotating the nut clockwise or anticlockwise?

....

b) Which rotates through the greatest distance: the turning force on the nut or the effort force?

....

4 A gardener wants to apply an effort force at the end of a lever to raise a load.

Diagrams A and B show two slightly different ways of positioning the lever, fulcrum, and load.

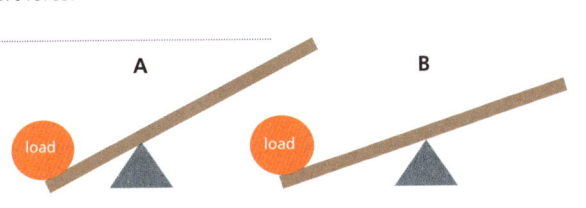

Which set up, A or B, would enable the gardener to raise the load with the smallest effort force?

Explain your answer.

....

Physics 69

ORGANISE 3: What is a moment?

Calculating moment

The turning effect of a force is called **moment**, and can be calculated using the following equation:

moment = size of force × distance from force to fulcrum

In this diagram, the effort force applied to the screwdriver creates a clockwise turning effect, which causes the lid of the paint tin to be levered off. This turning effect can be increased if a larger force is exerted or a longer screwdriver is used.

- The effort force applied to the screwdriver is 10 N.
- The distance from the rim of the tin to where the effort force is applied to the screwdriver is 0.16 m.
- So, moment = 10 × 0.16 = 1.6 Nm

> Moment is calculated by multiplying force in newtons by distance in metres. So, the unit for moment is Nm.

Exerting a pulling force on a door handle creates a turning effect, or moment, on the door. The door's hinges act as the fulcrum (or pivot). Here, the woman pulls the door handle with a force of 10 N. The distance from the handle to the hinges is 0.8 m. The moment (or turning effect) that opens the door is calculated as:

moment = 10 × 0.8 = 8 Nm

Applying the equation for moment to a see-saw

To demonstrate moments, we can create a model see-saw by balancing a metre rule on a triangular wooden block placed on a table. The wooden block acts as the fulcrum.

A 1 N weight is placed on the metre rule, 0.4 m from the fulcrum. The weight pushes down on the metre rule causing it to rotate clockwise.

clockwise moment = 1 × 0.4 = 0.4 Nm

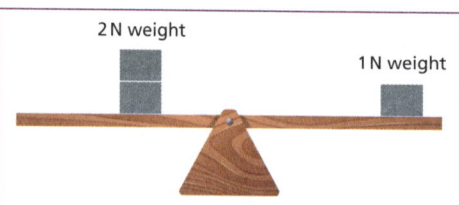

If we want to balance the model see-saw using a 2 N weight, the 2 N weight would need to be moved along the rule until it balances. The distance from the 2 N weight to the fulcrum is 0.2 m. The 2 N weight made the metre rule rotate in an anticlockwise direction until the metre rule was balanced:

anticlockwise moment = 2 × 0.2 = 0.4 Nm

> A see-saw is balanced when the clockwise moment is equal to the anticlockwise moment.

RETRIEVE
3) What is a moment?

Calculating moment

1) The spanner is being used as a lever by a plumber to tighten a nut on a bolt. The bolt acts as the fulcrum.

The force labelled F is the effort force. Distance L is the distance from the bolt to the effort force.

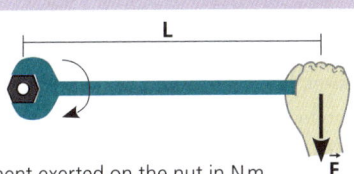

a) Force F = 20 N and length L = 0.3 m. Calculate the moment exerted on the nut in Nm.

.... Nm

b) If the plumber had grasped the spanner at its centre, 0.15 m from the bolt, what would be the moment created by the 20 N effort force?

.... Nm

Applying the equation for moment to a see-saw

2) The diagram shows a model see-saw. The letters A to E represent equally spaced points on the see-saw's beam.

a) Which letter represents the fulcrum? Tick the correct answer.

A ☐ B ☐ C ☐ D ☐ E ☐

b) Circle the correct word to complete the sentence.

If a weight was placed on the see-saw at point A, the see-saw would rotate **clockwise/ anticlockwise**.

c) If the weight at point A was 1 N, at what point would you put a 2 N weight to balance the see-saw?

....

3) The image shows two children on a see-saw.

a) The child on the left has a weight of 400 N. The distance from this child to the fulcrum is 1.5 m. Calculate the moment created by this child's weight.

.... Nm

b) When both children lift their feet off the ground, the left-hand side of the see-saw's beam touches the ground. Both children are 1.5 m from the fulcrum. What does this tell you about the weight of the child on the right?

....

c) The child on the left suddenly jumps off the see-saw. Does the see-saw turn clockwise or anticlockwise?

....

Physics 71

ORGANISE
3 · What is a machine?

What is the main purpose of a machine?

A machine is a device created by a person to make it easier to perform a specific task. Most homes have machines with either mechanical parts or electrical parts, or both, e.g. a washing machine or a food mixer. However, **simple machines** can also be found at home and at school.

The function of a simple machine is to change the size or direction of a force. It may have one, two or even zero moving parts. There are six types of simple machine:
- wheel and axle
- wedge
- lever
- pulley
- screw
- inclined plane.

Types and uses of simple machines

A **wheel and axle** can be used to raise a load, for example, a bucket containing water from a well. The wheel and axle are joined together. When the wheel is turned, the axle turns with it. The rope winds around the axle and raises the bucket. The force applied to rotate the wheel is smaller than the force needed to lift the bucket directly by hand.	
The head of the axe is in the shape of a **wedge**. When the axe is moved downwards at speed, the wedge re-directs the force outwards and splits the piece of wood.	
A bottle opener is a **lever**. The bottle opener enables the cap on the bottle to be removed with a small effort force.	
This single fixed **pulley** changes the direction of the force needed to lift a load. The load is lifted by pulling down on the rope. This means that you can use your own body weight to help you lift the load.	
A **screw** can be used to attach objects together and drill holes. Other objects with a screw thread include a bolt, jar lid, wine corkscrew, and a car jack. A screw thread changes a rotational force to a force acting in a straight line.	
Pushing the barrel up the **inclined plane** into the van requires a smaller force than if you tried to lift it directly in. An inclined plane is also known as a ramp.	

RETRIEVE 3 — What is a machine?

What is the main purpose of a machine?

1 **a)** Describe the function of a simple machine.
....

b) Name the six types of simple machine.
....
....

Types and uses of simple machines

2 The images below are examples of simple machines. Give the name of the type of simple machine that is shown in each image.

a) .... **b)** .... **c)** ....

d) .... **e)** .... **f)** ....

3 To be able to cut through material, the inner edges of these scissor blades are in the shape of a wedge. This is one type of simple machine. However, there is another type of simple machine in action with the scissors.

a) What is the other type of simple machine in the scissors?
....

b) Explain your answer to part a).
....
....

Physics 73

Mixed questions

1 Look at the diagram of *Amoeba*. *Amoeba* is a unicellular organism.

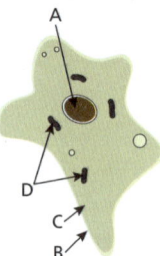

a) Write down the letter that labels each of these structures.

   i) nucleus

   ii) cytoplasm

   iii) the site of respiration

b) Draw labelled arrows on the diagram to show the movement of oxygen and carbon dioxide into or out of *Amoeba*.

2 The diagram below shows parts of the Periodic Table.

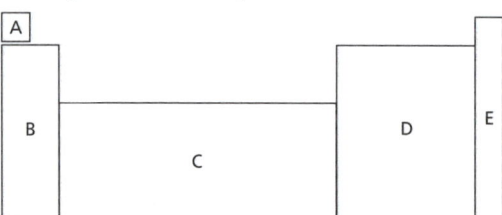

a) Write the letter that represents each of the following:

   i) transition metals

   ii) hydrogen

   iii) noble gases

b) What is listed on the Periodic Table?

....

c) Draw a particle diagram in the box to represent gold, a pure metal.

74

Mixed questions

3) The table shows nutrient details on the label of a packet of biscuits.

Figures for 100 grams of biscuits	
Energy	1000 kJ
Protein	9 grams
Carbohydrate	70 grams
Lipids	15 grams
Fibre	3 grams
Iron	2 milligrams
Vitamin D	1 microgram

a) Write down the nutrient in the table that is needed for each of these functions.

i) To control how fast food moves through the digestive system

....

ii) For repair and growth in the body

....

iii) To prevent anaemia

....

b) A person needs 11 000 kJ of energy in their diet each day.

Calculate how many biscuits they would need to eat to supply this energy. ....

....

c) Explain what would happen to the person if they ate more than this number of biscuits each day over a long period of time.

....

....

d) A person eats one of the biscuits.

Explain how the protein in the biscuit is physically and chemically digested in their body.

....

....

....

4) A bungee cord can be used to secure loads on a bicycle.

A student is investigating the effect a force has on a bungee cord. She sets up the apparatus so she can attach a weight to the end of the bungee. She uses the metre rule to make measurements of the bungee's length.

These are the student's measurements:
- length of bungee with no weight attached = 60 cm
- length of bungee with a 5 N weight attached = 82 cm
- length of bungee after the 5 N weight is removed = 60 cm

a) **i)** What is the name given to the increase in the bungee's length when it is stretched?

....

ii) Use the student's measurements to calculate the increase in the bungee's length.

Increase in length = ... cm

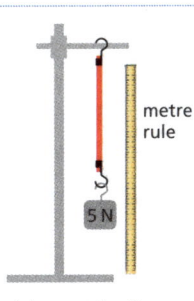

Mixed questions　75

Mixed questions

iii) Do the student's measurements show that the bungee is **elastic**? Explain your answer.

....

b) A much longer bungee is used for bungee jumping.

  i) At first, the bungee is slack and does not exert a force on the boy jumping. At this point in the jump the boy's speed is increasing. There are two forces acting on his body: weight and air resistance.

  Are these forces balanced? Explain your answer.

  ....

  ii) Add **two** labelled arrows to the diagram to represent air resistance and the boy's weight.

  iii) As the boy continues to fall, the bungee starts to stretch and exerts a force on the boy. The boy's speed decreases.

  What is the direction of the force exerted on the boy by the bungee? ....

5 The diagram shows a sperm cell about to fertilise an egg cell.

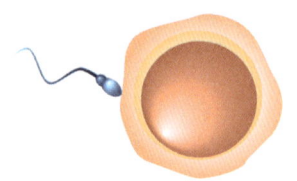

Answer these questions using words from this list.

| ovary | oviduct | sperm duct | testis | uterus | vagina |

a) Where was the sperm made? ....
b) Where was the egg made? ....
c) Where is the process of fertilisation happening? ....

6 a) The table shows some speed values in kilometres per hour for a woman walking and jogging.

Activity	walking	jogging
Speed in km/h	5	8

  i) How much time would it take her to walk 10 kilometres? .... hours

  ii) If she jogged for a $\frac{1}{2}$ hour, what distance would she travel? .... km

b) The woman heads to a track to go running. She completes 4 laps of the track in 10 minutes.

  i) Each lap of the track is 0.5 kilometres.
  What distance does she run?   distance = ... km

Mixed questions

ii) Divide the time taken in minutes by 60 to convert to hours.　　time = ... hours

iii) Calculate her running speed in kilometres per hour using the equation below:

speed = distance ÷ time　　　　　　　　　　　　　　　speed = ... km/h

iv) Is the speed value you calculated in part b) iii) her average speed or her actual speed at a point in her run? Explain your answer.

....

7 In a chemical change a new substance is made.

Complete the table to name each type of chemical reaction that is being described.

Name of the chemical change	Description
	Burning
	Adding oxygen
	Using heat to break down a substance
	Using electricity to break down a substance
	Breaking down of a substance
	When an acid and a base (alkali) react together

8 The diagram shows a model used to demonstrate breathing.

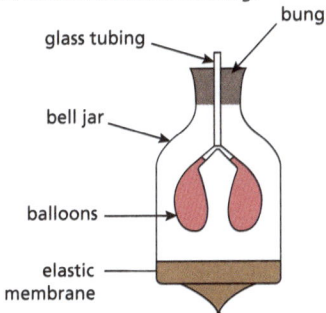

Labels: bung, glass tubing, bell jar, balloons, elastic membrane

a) Which parts of the model represent these structures?

　i) the lungs ....

　ii) the trachea ....

　iii) the diaphragm ....

b) Explain what would happen if the elastic membrane was pulled downwards.

....

....

....

Scientific skills

How is data collected?

Types of data

In a scientific **investigation** you will collect data. Data can be:
- **qualitative** – using your senses to make observations; this usually includes what you see, what you hear and what you smell
- **quantitative** – numbers and values that you have read and recorded from measuring instruments.

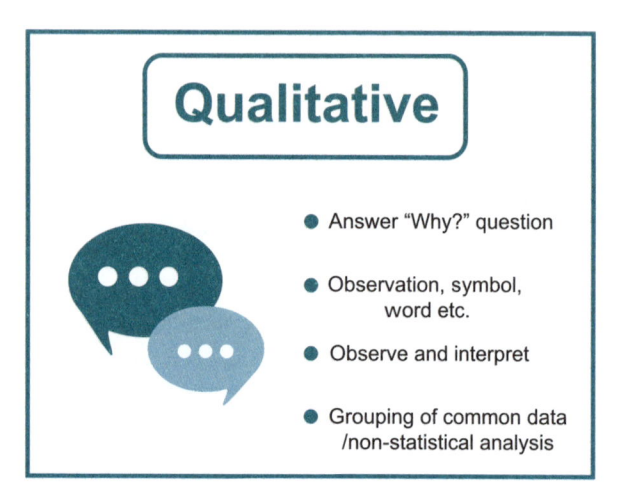

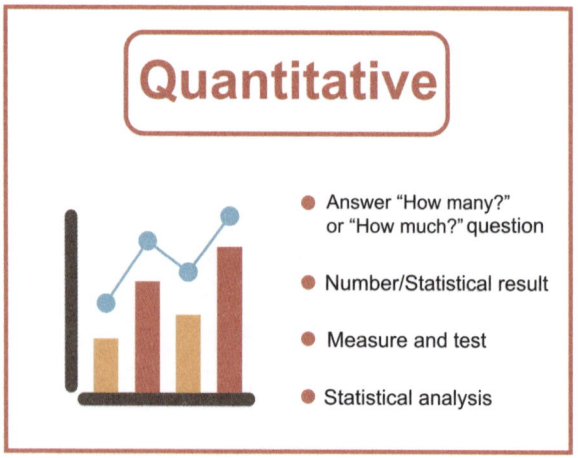

Qualitative
- Answer "Why?" question
- Observation, symbol, word etc.
- Observe and interpret
- Grouping of common data /non-statistical analysis

Quantitative
- Answer "How many?" or "How much?" question
- Number/Statistical result
- Measure and test
- Statistical analysis

Scientists prefer to collect quantitative data because it is:
- **reliable** – each time the investigation is repeated, similar results are collected
- **objective** – the data is not influenced by how the person is feeling
- **useful** – graphs and charts can be made which allow **predictions** outside the data that has been collected.

Scientific skills

Measuring equipment

When you are choosing to measure quantities it is important to choose the correct measuring equipment. This means using equipment that:
- has the **correct range** – the equipment can measure all the values that you need for your investigation
- is **accurate** – the value measured is close to the true value
- has suitable **interval** and **resolution** – the equipment can detect the changes and you can read the values.

> Choose a measuring instrument that has the biggest interval and the smallest range for what you are trying to measure, so that you get the most accurate measurement. For example, to measure 10 ml of water you would use a 10 ml measuring cylinder, rather than using a 100 ml measuring cylinder or filling up a 1 ml measuring cylinder ten times.

Quantity to be measured	Measuring equipment
Volume – measure the volume at the bottom of the meniscus and in your eye line.	Measuring cylinder
Temperature – make sure the bulb of the thermometer is in the substance you want to take the temperature of.	Thermometer
Time – remember to choose seconds or minutes to record your time. 1:30 on a stopwatch is 1 minute and 30 seconds, which is 90 seconds or 1.5 minutes.	Stopwatch
Top pan balance – scales are used in kitchens and bathrooms to measure mass. In a lab, a top pan balance is used.	Top pan balance

Scientific skills 79

Scientific skills

What makes good data?

Scientific method

Science is the study of the physical and natural world through **observation** and **experiment**. The **scientific method** is the way that scientists work in a **systematic approach**.

At the start of an investigation, you should set out what you want to find out in your investigation; this is often a question. All of the **data** that you collect in your investigation should help you answer the question and is called **valid** data.

There is no need to collect data that doesn't help you answer the question. For example, if you wanted to know the average height of your classmates you need to collect quantitative data of their heights, but you do not need to collect data on their hair colour as hair colour is not valid data that would help you answer your aim.

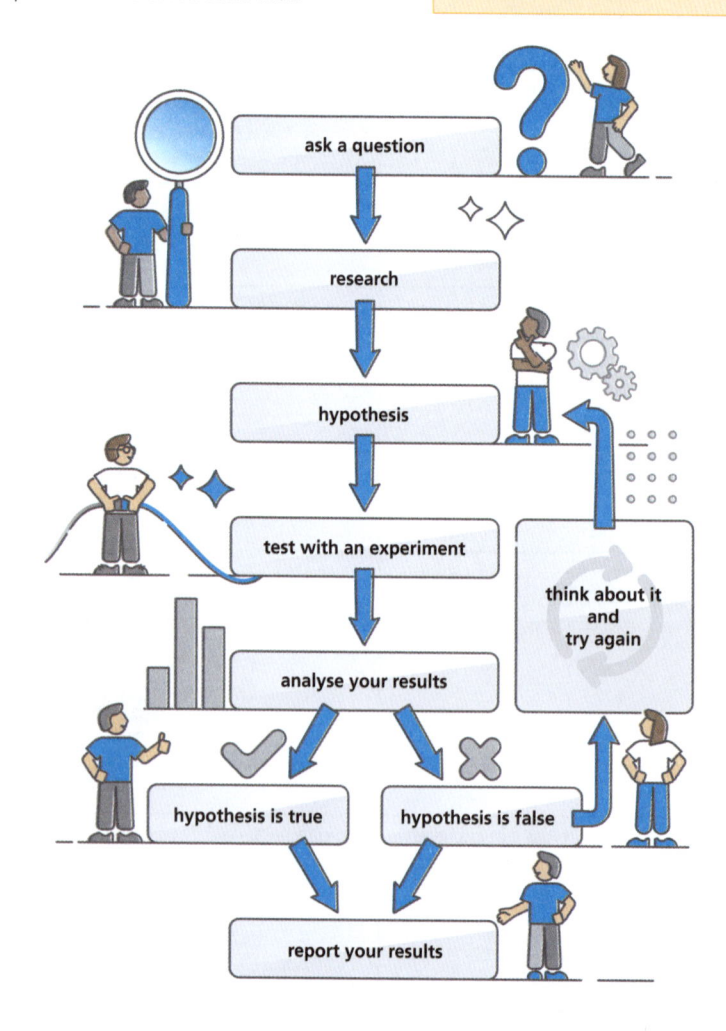

- ask a question
- research
- hypothesis
- test with an experiment
- analyse your results
- hypothesis is true
- hypothesis is false
- think about it and try again
- report your results

Scientific skills

Good data

Scientists want to collect **accurate** data that is close to the true value. But they also want their investigations to produce **reliable** data (data that is similar each time the experiment is repeated).

Imagine if every time you threw a dart at a dartboard you got the bullseye. You would be both reliable and accurate in your throwing.

But if sometimes you hit the bullseye and sometimes you do not, then you are sometimes accurate but you are not reliable.

Averages

Often, three sets of data are collected for each experiment. If all the values are similar, then the data is reliable. But if a value is not similar you should disregard it as an **anomaly**. There will still be some variation in the results so it is usually worthwhile calculating the **average**.

Mean or average	Median
the sum of the numbers divided by the amount of numbers	the number in the middle
5 + 5 + 5 + 6 + 7 + 7 + 14	5 5 5 ⑥ 7 7 14
49/7 = ⑦	(numbers must be in ascending order)

Mode	Range
the number that appears the most	the difference between the greatest and smallest number
⑤⑤⑤ 6 7 7 14	5 5 5 6 7 7 14
	14 − 5 = ⑨

Answers

Biology

Page 5
1. a) A b) C c) D d) C
2. This is where respiration occurs to release energy.
3. cellulose
4. to support the cell
5. cell wall, vacuole
6. They are underground, so do not receive any light.
7. a) The tail allows it to swim to the egg so it can fertilise it.
   b) The projection increases the surface area for absorbing water and minerals.
8. Specialised cells only do certain jobs and so are more efficient.

Page 7
1. Cells are too small to see with the naked eye.
2. a) A b) F c) B d) C
3. a) (microscope) slide b) stain c) cover slip
4. The lines are sketchy; The cell is shaded.
5. 40 000 micrometres
6. 40 000 ÷ 40 = 1000

Page 9
1. nucleus, mitochondria
2. in the cytoplasm
3. a) Paramecium b) yeast c) Euglena d) bacteria
4. Euglena, Paramecium, yeast
5. cells, tissues, organs, systems
6. Sperm – cell; The femur – organ; The heart – organ; A neurone – cell; Heart muscle – tissue

Page 11
1. a) stamen b) carpel c) anther d) ovule
2. the male gamete
3. the transfer of pollen from the anther to the stigma
4. to attract insects
5. produce nectar/have scent/produce sticky pollen/anthers or stigmas are inside the flower
6. They make large amounts to increase the chance of reaching a stigma and are light to get carried by the wind.
7. Stigma/anthers hang outside the flower.
8. tube; ovule; seed; ovary
9. So that the new plants do not compete with each other or the parent.
10. They are carried by the wind as they are very light.

Page 13
1. a) ovary b) cervix c) vagina
2. oviducts (fallopian tubes)
3. The sperm and egg will not be able to meet so fertilisation cannot occur.
4. sperm
5. a) Produce sperm. b) Protects the testes and keeps them below body temperature.
6. Changes that occur in young teenagers to prepare them for reproduction.
7. Growth of hair under the armpits/around the reproductive organs.
8. The release of an egg from the ovary.
9. 28 days
10. Ovulation usually occurs around day 14 so this increases the chance of a sperm and egg meeting.

Page 15
1. 38 weeks
2. It has divided to form a two-celled embryo.
3. It is a ball of cells surrounded by a protective coat.
4. It grows larger.
5. a) D b) G c) B
6. by the umbilical cord
7. to protect the baby
8. a) supplies nutrients to the placenta/foetus
   b) contracts to push the baby out during birth

Page 17
1. To store energy.

Answers

2. rice (or other suitable answer)
3. a) Milk contains most of the nutrients needed.
   b) Milk does not contain fibre.
4. A diet that contains the correct amount of all the food nutrients.
5. a) 1500 kJ
   b) They need more energy to enable their muscles to contract for running.
   c) $\frac{2000}{12000} = \frac{1}{6}$ (17%)
6. emulsion test
7. Heat it with Benedict's reagent. It should turn orange-red if sugar is present.
8. purple/violet

Page 19
1. a) H b) E c) D d) C
2. The small intestine is narrow and the large intestine is wide.
3.

	Physical digestion	Chemical digestion
Enzymes in the stomach digesting protein		✓
Starch being broken down by saliva		✓
Food being churned in the stomach	✓	
Teeth chewing food	✓	

4. in the small intestine
5. pancreas, salivary glands, stomach
6. so the digested food can easily pass into the bloodstream
7. to absorb water to make semi-solid faeces

Page 21
1. a) B b) A c) E
2. to keep it open
3. thin wall; close to blood vessels; large numbers so large surface area
4. trachea, bronchus, bronchioles, alveoli
5. intercostal muscles and diaphragm
6. Breathing is the process of moving air in and out of the lungs but respiration releases energy from food.
7. Muscles in the bronchioles contract, which makes the tubes narrower.
8. dust/pollen/pet hairs/cigarette smoke

Page 23
1. Arrow drawn from right to left.
2. It would speed up.
3. Changes in temperature change the speed that molecules move.
4.

Substance	Diffuses in	Diffuses out
Oxygen	✓	
Carbon dioxide		✓
Glucose	✓	

5. respiration
6. alveoli; blood; large; thin
7. They take away the digested food molecules and so increase the speed of diffusion.

Page 25
1. a) vitamin C b) iron c) vitamin D/calcium
2. a) lettuce b) meat c) eggs
3. painful joints/heart disease/high blood pressure/difficulties with breathing/diabetes
4. Exercise requires energy and so more body fat is used up to release this energy.
5. They decrease in size.
6. Addictive means that the body will want the effects from smoking more cigarettes.
7. nicotine
8. a) tar b) nicotine
9. It reduces the amount of oxygen that can be carried by the blood.

Answers

Chemistry

Page 27
1. Risk – How likely the dangers are to cause a problem; Hazard – The dangers; Risk assessment – Evaluating the hazards and risks, giving ideas to reduce them and what to do if there is a problem
2. goggles; eye protection
3. Flammable
4. gloves; eye protection; goggles
5. Close the air hole to ensure that the flame is orange (which is more easily seen and therefore less likely to cause an accident).
6. air hole open, blue flame, top of gas cone
7. to prevent the hair from catching fire

Page 29
1. a) False b) True c) True d) True e) False
2. test tube, water, sand, beaker, heat
3. folded filter paper, residue, funnel, filtrate
4. The first column is the independent variable and the values are chosen in the method.
5.
Person	Handspan (cm)
Jan	
Janna	
Janine	

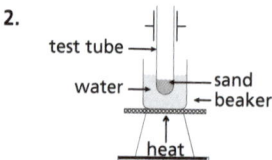

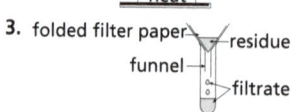

Page 31
1. Just oxygen atoms/molecules/particles.
2. 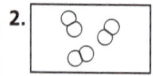
3. one
4. Periodic Table
5. Two or more
6. carbon and oxygen
7. a) False b) True c) False d) True e) True

Page 33
1. It stays the same.
2. Salt – Solute; Water – Solvent; Salty water – Solution
3. A colourless/clear liquid is made.
4. The solute particles/molecules separate from each other and fit into the gaps between the solvent particles/molecules to form a mixture called a solution.
5. 28g
6. It increases as temperature increases.
7. insoluble
8. Below 0°C, water is a solid and above 100°C, water is a gas. Solvents are usually liquids and so water can only be found as a liquid between these temperature values.

Page 35
1. physical
2. Insoluble – Does not dissolve in the solvent; Immiscible – Does not mix; Soluble – Dissolves in the solvent
3. using a separating funnel/decanting
4. distillation
5. folded filter paper, residue/charcoal, funnel, filtrate/water
6. Lose water to the atmosphere – Evaporation, Distillation; Collect pure water – Distillation; Collect large salt crystals – Crystallisation; Collect small salt crystals – Evaporation

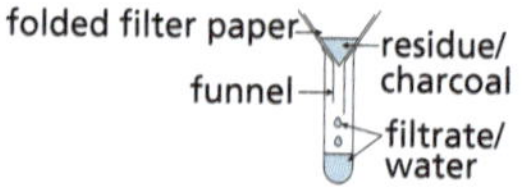

Page 37
1. sodium chloride
2. Pump the water into salt pans/shallow ponds, leave the water to evaporate, collect the salt crystals.

Answers

3. a) False **b)** False **c)** True
4. brown/yellow/red
5. mining or solution mining
6. Gritting roads/Extracting pure salt for cooking/Preserving food/Adding taste to food
7. Dissolve the rock salt, filter out the impurities, crystallise/evaporate the filtrate.
8. solutions with more than one solute
9. Purify alcoholic drinks/Separate the gases in the air/Separate the different fuels in crude oil

Page 39
1. Dmitri Mendeleev
2. periods
3. groups
4. a) False **b)** True **c)** True
5. a) Au **b)** 79 **c)** 197 **d)** transition metal

Page 41
1. It is sonorous.
2. It is a conductor of electricity/It is ductile.
3. Gold, Au – Mined as a native metal; Aluminium, Al – Electrolysis; Iron, Fe – Reduction with carbon, C.
4. A metal made by combining two or more other metals.
5. steel
6. orange/yellow
7. a) barium/Ba **b)** potassium/K

Page 43
1. acidic non-metal oxides
2. on the right
3. a) True **b)** True **c)** False **d)** False **e)** False
4. When an element can arrange its atoms in more than one structure.
5. helium/argon/neon/krypton/xenon/radon
6. between the metals and the non-metals
7. electronics
8. boron/B; silicon/Si; germanium/Ge; arsenic/As; antimony/Sb; tellurium/Te; polonium/Po; astatine/At

Page 45
1. a) chemical change, physical change **b)** physical change **c)** chemical change **d)** chemical change, physical change
2. A gas is being made.
3. Atoms in the starting chemicals rearrange to make a new substance. No atoms are created or destroyed, they are just rearranged.
4. 20g
5. 16g
6. Rust is a compound made between iron and oxygen. The iron nail gained oxygen from the air to make the rust. So, the mass increased.

Page 47
1. starting substances in a chemical reaction
2. substances made in a chemical reaction
3. ● + ●● → ●●●
4. copper + oxygen → copper oxide
5. copper carbonate → copper oxide + carbon dioxide
6. a) True **b)** False **c)** True **d)** False **e)** False

Page 49
1. A chemical reaction where oxygen is added.
2. magnesium + oxygen → magnesium oxide
3. 20%
4. copper + oxygen → copper oxide
5. ethanol + oxygen → carbon dioxide + water
6. a), **b)**, **c)** and **e)**
7. heating/cooking
8. oxides

Page 51
1. A new substance is made.
2. heat/Bunsen burner
3. carbon and oxygen
4. lead carbonate → lead oxide + carbon dioxide
5. calcium hydroxide solution
6. Heating the calcium carbonate – Chemical change; Adding water to calcium oxide – Chemical change; Adding water to solid calcium hydroxide to make a solution –

Answers 85

Answers

Physical change; Filtering the mixture to collect the filtrate of calcium hydroxide – Physical change

Page 53
1. physical change
2. chemical change
3. g/grams
4. a) False b) True c) True d) True
5. reactants; products; none; atoms
6. g/cm^3
7. 10.5 g/cm^3

Physics

Page 55
1. Any suitable example such as pushing a shopping trolley, pushing a pram.
2. Any suitable example such as pulling a door handle to open or close a door, pulling a rope in a tug of war.
3. increasing the object's speed; decreasing the object's speed; changing the object's shape
4. a) newton
   b) N
   c) newton-meter (or spring balance)
5. The 10 N arrow would be longer than (twice as long as) the 5 N arrow.
6. **A:** left; **B:** right; **C:** right
7. The trolley does not move.

Page 57
1. Mass is determined by the amount of matter in the object. The amount of matter depends on the number of particles/atoms/molecules.
2. kilograms, kg
3. a) weight b) newton, N
4. a) contact force
   b) gravitational force/gravity/weight
   c) arrow drawn downwards from the middle of the box
5. a) Her mass on the Moon is still 60 kg.
   Her weight on the Moon is less than 600 N because the Moon's gravity is weaker.
   b) Venus

Page 59
1. a) the weight of the cyclist and his bicycle
   b) The driving force and the drag force are the same size but act in opposite directions.

2. a) Weight must be larger than the drag force because her speed is increasing.
   b) balanced forces
3. A contact force of 500 N acts towards the car.

Page 61
1. squashing/bending/twisting
2. Measure the length of the spring. Attach the mass to the spring. Measure the new length of the spring. Subtract the original length from the new length to get the extension.
3. Measure the length of the spring. Remove the three masses from above the spring. Measure the new length of the spring. Subtract the original length from the new length to get the compression.
4. Doubling the stretching force doubles the extension.
5. a) Material B
   b) Material B's graph is a straight line passing through the origin.

Page 63
1. attraction between molecules in the two surfaces/roughness of the two surfaces
2. water resistance
3. air resistance
4. a) Useful; because it helps to prevent the cyclist's shoes from slipping off the pedals.
   b) Not useful; because it opposes the cyclist's motion. c) Not useful; because it causes damage. d) Useful; because it prevents the cyclist's hands from slipping off the handlebars.
5. The boat is given a streamlined shape.
6. the grip on the soles of the shoes
7. oil

Answers

8. A tyre with a tread less than 1.6 mm is more likely to skid.

Page 65

1. a) X: air resistance; **Y:** weight/gravitational force/gravity

b) Y

c) Speeding up. The forces are not balanced.

d) X: changes direction; **Y:** does not change direction

2. a) arrow from the dart pointing vertically downwards

b) No; The dart will hit below the centre of the dartboard because of the force of gravity.

Page 67

1. a) 90 km/h

b) actual speed

2. total distance = 22 + 22 = 44 km

3. distance is half of 4, which is 2 miles

4. distance = 50 + 50 = 100 cm

5. average speed = 200 ÷ 20 = 10 m/s

6. average speed = 200 ÷ 4 = 50 km/h

7. a) 1.8 × 1000 = 1800 m

b) 5 × 60 = 300 s

c) average speed = 1800 ÷ 300 = 6 m/s

8. Average speed considers the whole journey. Actual speed is the speed at a point in time.

Page 69

1. a) [diagram: wooden beam balanced on pivot with load at X]

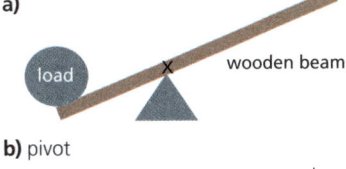

b) pivot

c) [diagram: wooden beam tilted with load]

2. a) [diagram of hammer with effort and load labelled]

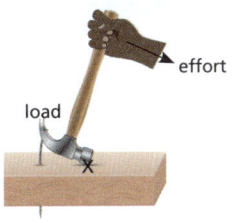

b) the effort

3. a) anticlockwise

b) the effort force

4. A; because the load is closest to the pivot and the effort is furthest from the pivot.

Page 71

1. a) moment = 20 × 0.3 = 6 Nm

b) moment = 20 × 0.15 = 3 Nm

2. a) C

b) anticlockwise

c) D

3. a) moment = 400 × 1.5 = 600 Nm

b) The weight of the child on the right is less than 400 N/less than the weight of the child on the left.

c) clockwise

Page 73

1. a) to change the size or direction of a force

b) wheel and axle; wedge; lever; pulley; screw; inclined plane

2. a) wheel and axle **b)** ramp **c)** screw **d)** pulley **e)** wedge **f)** lever

3. a) lever

b) There is a pivot (fulcrum) in the middle of the scissors.

Answers 87

Answers

Mixed questions

Pages 74–77

1. **a) i)** A **ii)** C **iii)** D
   b) [diagram of amoeba with labels A, B, C, D, oxygen, carbon dioxide]

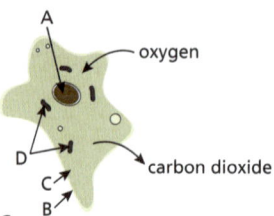

2. **a) i)** C
   ii) A
   iii) E
   b) elements
   c) [diagram of particles arranged in a grid]

3. **a) i)** fibre **ii)** protein **iii)** iron
   b) 11 000 ÷ 1000 = 11 biscuits
   c) They would take in too much energy which would be stored as fat. They would become overweight/obese.
   d) Physically digested by chewing in the mouth by the teeth and by churning in the stomach. Chemically digested by enzymes released in the stomach.

4. **a) i)** extension
   ii) increase in length = 82 − 60 = 22 cm
   iii) The bungee is elastic because it returns to its original length when the weight is removed.
   b) i) The forces are not balanced because the boy's speed is increasing/changing.
   ii) [diagram of bungee jumper with arrows labelled air resistance (up) and weight (down)] Note that the weight arrow is longer than the air resistance arrow.
   iii) upwards

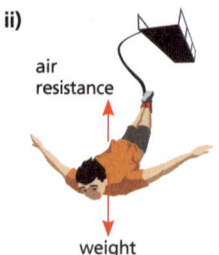

5. **a)** testis **b)** ovary **c)** oviduct

6. **a) i)** 2 hours
   ii) 4 km
   b) i) distance = 4 × 0.5 = 2 km
   ii) time = 10 ÷ 60 = 0.167 hours
   iii) speed = 2 ÷ 0.167 = 12 km/h
   iv) It is her average speed because it is the total distance value used in the equation.

7.

Name of the chemical change	Description
Combustion	Burning
Oxidation	Adding oxygen
Thermal decomposition	Using heat to break down a substance
Electrolysis	Using electricity to break down a substance
Decomposition	Breaking down of a substance
Neutralisation	When an acid and a base (alkali) react together

8. **a) i)** balloons **ii)** glass tubing
   iii) elastic membrane
   b) The volume inside the jar would increase and the pressure would decrease. This would cause air to pass into the balloons which would inflate.